AF350309

Additional Praise for The Beloved Republic

Steven Harvey always writes with elegance, kindness, and a seemingly fathomless generosity. In his humane and magisterial collection of essays, *The Beloved Republic*, he offers readers even more. His beautiful writing aches for what is ailing us, but he doesn't simply leave us aching. He offers readers a balm of love for ourselves and each other. Whether he's writing about a mother's suicide, racial unrest, American politics, or an attempt to save a beached whale, Steven Harvey reminds us of our shared humanity, and reveals paths of redemption.

—Joe Mackall, author of *Plain Secrets: An Outsider among the Amish*

Steven Harvey's elegant essays in *The Beloved Republic* span centuries and continents, guiding us from a third century poetry-writing celebration at the Orchid Pavilion to the 2017 Neo-Nazi violence that erupted in Charlottesville, Virginia. Harvey's generosity to his readers grows with every page, his warm, thoughtful presence inviting us not only into his own domestic sphere of family, home, and music, but also into the worlds of scientists, writers, artists, philosophers, mathematicians, and religious, cultural, and political icons. He offers no answers, only deeply observed questions that take us deeper and deeper into the mysteries of this twinned world we inhabit, one populated by "tyrants, thugs, and loud-mouth bullies," yes, but also by a "peaceful and fragile confederacy of kind, benevolent, and creative people," the beloved republic Harvey invites us all to become part of.

—Rebecca McClanahan, author of *In the Key of New York City: A Memoir in Essays* and *The Tribal Knot: A Memoir of Family, Community, and a Century of Change*

The Beloved Republic should be required reading for all of us. With his gentle, sanguine essays, Steven Harvey reinvigorates me with hope that all is not lost, that goodness will prevail, that art and literature and music continue to move people to love and kindness.

—Patrick Madden, author of *Disparities: Essays*

Steven Harvey explores the many ways that a love of words, natural beauty, books, music, creativity and decency can transform a world of struggle into his "beloved republic." A master of the personal/political essay, Harvey reveals how moments of darkness—be it racial issues, a mother's suicide, a dying beached whale--can lead to light. Often a reliable cup of steaming pre-dawn coffee makes the difference.

—Mimi Schwartz, author if *Good Neighbors, Bad Times Revisited*

In the hands of a skillful writer, the essay allows for the posing and pondering of life's essential questions without settling for easy answers. Steven Harvey is a consummately skillful writer, as he demonstrates in each of these searching, often wrenching essays, whose subjects range from racial divides to his mother's suicide, from mountain music to the mystery of consciousness. These pages reveal the truth of his claim that an author's voice "can bring the solace of comradery to a reader." We are not alone, he assures us, in our fear, bewilderment, or wonder.

—Scott Russell Sanders, author of *The Way of Imagination*

I would follow the narrator of the essays in Steven Harvey's *The Beloved Republic* anywhere—and I do: into the water to lay hands on a beached sperm whale, through the classroom doors to teach *Beowulf* in the wake of the September 11th attacks, or under the stairs of his childhood home after his mother's suicide where the nails poke through: "Like stars they glittered in the crawl space, and I looked into them as I listened to the groan in the floorboards." Steven Harvey is an essayist's essayist, a writer's writer, a reader's writer. These urgent and gorgeous essays help us to make sense of this broken and beautiful world with compassion, wisdom, love, and art. Steven Harvey is one of our best. What can I say? I needed this book.

—Jill Christman, author of *If This Were Fiction: A Love Story in Essays*

The ease and grace of Harvey's prose belies the big issues he tackles – race, politics, culture. And, in his personal life, a mother who committed suicide, a brilliant student who cuts herself, and a keen awareness of approaching mortality. This book, perfect for its time, puzzles over questions about where we fit in the upheaval all around us and does not give up on the possibility of a more luminous humanity. Harvey's mind and heart work in tandem in these thoughtfully emotional essays. If only those in our halls of power had half this much intelligence and empathy!

—Sue William Silverman, author, *How to Survive Death and Other Inconveniences*

Steven Harvey's *The Beloved Republic* is a masterful collection of essays, provocative, always engaging, a compelling journey from page to page. Harvey tackles challenging issues, societal and personal, with intelligence and compassion. Yes, our beloved republic is under siege, but these thoughtful "dispatches" ultimately offer hope and beauty.

—Dinty W. Moore, author of *Between Panic & Desire*

Steven Harvey has written a remarkable, gently urgent, and poignantly beautiful book with the vibrant power to lend courage and spiritual sustenance in the difficult times we face. This is a book to treasure, to return to for reflection and guidance, and to give away: to remind all citizens of the Beloved Republic of the ties that anchor us together.

—Sonya Huber, author of *Supremely Tiny Acts: A Memoir of a Day*

Welcome, intimates. Open your palms to cradle this book inside which resides "the solace of comradery." We need heartening daily, Harvey knows, having written "The Book of Knowledge" and offered it here among the resources and character models. Exemplars like Madre Luz who have been "beaten, toppled, and thrown to the ground only to rise again," comport the bow that tugs toward justice. We need her story as we need ears attuned "to the music in the air" to make such efforts, more than moral, comely. *The Beloved Republic* is a whale of a find. Like the beached giant onto which Harvey lays his hands alongside many kindred strangers, these essays demonstrate that nothing can be lost which has been drawn together.

—Amy Wright, author of *Paper Concert*

Also by Steven Harvey

A Geometry of Lilies

Lost in Translation

Bound for Shady Grove

The Book of Knowledge and Wonder

Folly Beach

The Beloved Republic

ESSAYS

STEVEN HARVEY

Wandering Aengus Press

Eastsound, Washington

First Edition. Published by Wandering Aengus Press

Nonfiction
ISBN: 979-8-218-00672-3
Author Photo: Namrata Harvey
Book Design: Jill McCabe Johnson

Wandering Aengus Press
PO Box 334 Eastsound, WA 98245
wanderingaenguspress.com

Wandering Aengus Press is dedicated to publishing works to enrich lives and make the world a better place.

TABLE OF CONTENTS

Introduction

A Whole Life | 2

I. The Beloved Republic

The Beloved Republic | 7

The Other Steve Harvey | 21

Madre Luz | 35

One Boy's Luminous Skin | 47

The Arc of the Universe | 50

Eclipsing the Brand | 63

Gatherin' Around J. P. Fraley | 75

The Political Personal Essay | 84

A Laying on of Hands | 98

II. Blood Mountain

Blood Mountain | 113

Orphaned Souls | 122

The Razor Blade | 132

Living Midnight | 140

Ya Mismo | 151

The Book of Knowledge | 165

A Vow of Poverty | 196

Kindly Dark | 208

Gratitude | 214

Acknowledgments | 216

About the Author | 218

The Beloved Republic

A Whole Life

The beech tree rising in our bow window finds its own shape without any help from me. It is a gift from my friend, the artist and naturalist Dale Cochran, who walked the woods with me before I built my house spotting which trees to keep. "Definitely that one," he said pointing to the healthy beech sapling with a split trunk, each one about as wide as my arm, that I have watched bulk up mightily over the years. He was right. In the summer it sprouts lovely, light-green leaves that turn coppery in the winter and rattle in the wind, and the bark is a smooth gray with scars that mark any blow it has taken. The word "book" can be traced back to beech tablets where the ancients carved sacred texts in runes, and in German and other modern European languages the word for book and beech are the same. As I wrote the essays that eventually filled the collection called *The Beloved Republic*, the tree inspired me.

The Beloved Republic began as separate essays that over a quarter century of writing became a book. While I worked on it, I raised four children and enjoyed five grandchildren with one more on the way, taught at one college, played in one musical group with whom I still perform, and lived with my wife in this house where I have spent nearly half of my life. The book had no predetermined focus. While I wrote it, I became who I am, and it tagged along, and in the shadow of the tree that looms overheard, I slowly discovered what it was about. The essay as a form began in this desultory way, as a loose collection on random subjects that Michel de

Montaigne called *essais*, the French word for attempts. Some of the finest collections in the past likewise grew organically out of the author's life finding their shape over time. Many, like mine, began as magazine pieces and later, almost as an afterthought, were collected in books. This kind of nonfiction miscellany has fallen out of fashion, I fear. Contemporary readers and publishers apparently prefer a focused book that drives home one idea, predetermined or discovered early by the writer. These focused collections take the shape that the author consciously gives them in advance. Thoreau's *Walden* with its theme of living deliberately boldly announced in its first essay is an example.

What I admire about the miscellany is that it is held together not by a vision, discovered early and pursued single-mindedly, but by a whole life. As essayists put together such collections written over decades, they do not explore a concept or a set of related concepts; rather, they reveal who they are, and, perhaps, why they are here. Like the beech, they grow into themselves over time. It is not easy for the reader who has to begin anew with each essay and in this the miscellany is much like a book of poems, meant to be read slowly, but as in poetry, the rewards can be great as reader joins writer on a quest to discover willy-nilly what one life is about. There is an intimacy in this method, a sense that the parts are cherished, glowing by their own light without ulterior motive.

But if the writer is lucky, the sum is greater than its parts, and a vision, as well as a life, can emerge, and that is what happened for me in my book. The glue, the ultimately unifying discovery of *The Beloved Republic*, is the old idea that creativity is valuable in itself, a view that goes in and out of favor. In an age when the planet and its people face unthinkable, unspeakable horrors, the need for social relevance is obvious, but as I wrote, I discovered that art generates meaning and offers beauty to a troubled planet, and in its very freshness, is profoundly spiritual and political. It generally brings out the best in us and helps us weather evil. Those who do this work form the "Beloved Republic," a phrase E. M. Forster coined for the peaceful and fragile confederacy of kind, benevolent, and creative people in a world of tyrants, thugs, and loud-mouthed bullies. They form an invincible army of losers in the service of love. My book slowly opening in surprises over decades can be read as dispatches from this beleaguered land. It grew into the idea and, like the beech, took its own, sweet time.

I. The Beloved Republic

So two cheers for Democracy: one because it admits variety and two because it permits criticism. Two cheers are quite enough: there is no occasion to give three. Only Love, the Beloved Republic, deserves that… Its members are to be found in all nations and classes, and all through the ages, and there is a secret understanding between them when they meet. They represent the true human tradition, the one permanent victory of our queer race over cruelty and chaos…. Their temple, as one of them remarked, is the holiness of the Heart's affections, and their kingdom, though they never possess it, is the wide-open world.

—E. M. Forster, "What I Believe"

THE BELOVED REPUBLIC

In the shade of the Orchid Pavilion on KuiJi Mountain, Wang Xizhi and guests gathered to purge evil from their lives. More than sixteen hundred years ago, young and old partied against a backdrop of upland ridges, steep peaks, abundant forests, and groves of towering bamboo. Clear creeks glittered, rippling past the pavilion, the winding streams carrying candlelit cups of wine to those who lined the bank. When a cup arrived, the guest who drank from it composed a poem on the spot. Even without pipes or pipa to play, the poets were happy sharing wine at creekside, content to find words to match their feelings.

Wang Xizhi, the most famous calligrapher of all time, wrote his *Preface to the Poems Composed at the Orchid Pavilion* that day while drinking wine himself, using his distinctive running script, the brush never leaving the page as he shaped each character with lines looping playfully or darkening by turns. When he thought about someone in the future writing about him and his friends long dead, the brush slipped so he blotted out the mistake, an error prized for its sincerity. Forming the characters *bei fu* for the bereaved he turned maudlin at the thought of all those loved ones long gone and stained the rice paper with his heavy stroke. Later he copied the *Preface* while sober but was unable to reproduce lines with the original emotions of that day centuries ago when the sky above the Orchid Pavilion was bright, the air clear, and a chance breeze delighted him and his guests. With a bountiful earth spread before them, the tipsy poets gazed into an expanding universe giddy, the outer world mirroring their joy. Cheeks flush with wine, they composed in a rush seeking words worthy of a day spent beside the rippling border of the Beloved Republic.

~   ~   ~

The Beloved Republic is the peaceful and fragile confederacy of kind, benevolent, and creative people that is necessary for civilized life in a world of tyrants, thugs, and loud-mouth bullies. During the darkest times, it sheds light and keeps us civil. Though the Beloved Republic has always been with us, E. M. Forster named and defined it in the essay "What I Believe" in 1939 when it was most under threat, putting his faith in the "natural warmth" of its happy and mutual reliability during the worst of times. "Tolerance, good temper, and sympathy" are its traits which, as Nazi Germany loomed, were "no stronger than a flower, battered beneath a military jackboot," an image fast becoming a cliché for the hobnailed crunch of German conquest and occupation. In a radio address before the war started, Forster explained that "thousands and thousands of innocent people" had been "killed, robbed, mutilated, insulted," and "imprisoned." Millions more would follow. News reports of book burnings at the University of Berlin and the mass deportation of Jews prefigured the "Age of Bloodshed" that Hitler's fanaticism would bring to Europe and the world. Against this backdrop of atrocity Forster argued for the existence, and persistence, of the Beloved Republic.

I don't remember the first time I read "What I Believe," but I do know the time that it brought the most comfort to me. It was after the election of Donald Trump in 2016. I had entered election night, like almost everyone, expecting a victory for common sense. We had long ago given up buying champagne after Al Gore's loss in 2000 when a bottle of it went bad after eight years of waiting, but we were anticipating popcorn for sure. Then around 10:30 Trump won Ohio and the calls from my kids started rolling in, each beginning with an identical *Dad?!* I use the interrobang to indicate the mixture of incredulity and indignation in their voices. It came across over the phone like an accusation: Everything you ever taught us about America is coming apart, *Dad.* While I was reassuring them that it was still early and we had the blue firewall in the upper Midwest, Trump went on a roll: North Carolina, Utah, Iowa. I particularly remember telling my angry and hurt daughter Alice not to worry. We still had Pennsylvania which the Republicans almost never win. Then, a little after 1:35, Trump won Pennsylvania, and was ahead in Wisconsin, Michigan, and Arizona.

I went to bed defeated and a little terrified, and when I woke the next morning Trump had won. The country had elected an authoritarian who modeled himself after Vladimir Putin to be President of the United States. A day or two later, still feeling vanquished and vulnerable—dazed, really—I looked up *Two Cheers for Democracy* and turned to "What I Believe."

Forster claims that the Beloved Republic can be found everywhere, its citizens easily recognizable. They are not heroes or saviors or politicians who exude "iron will, personal magnetism, dash, flair," and "sexlessness." It does not consist of special people, but of ordinary folks with a creative, rather than destructive, bent. Forster describes this band of true friends this way: "Not an aristocracy of power, based upon rank and influence, but an aristocracy of the sensitive, the considerate, and the plucky." Yes, I thought nodding in recognition. These people, he writes, amplifying on the idea, "are sensitive for others as well as for themselves, they are considerate without being fussy, their pluck is not swankiness but the power to endure, and they can take a joke." I thought about the inability of the President-in-waiting to take a joke, and knew that Forster had predicted it all, and then he offered a paradox that is both terrifying and comforting in its simple truth: The Beloved Republic make up "an invincible army, yet not a victorious one."

~　~　~

This invincible army of losers in the service of art, love, and friendship was famously on display on August 28 in 1963 during the March on Washington. The event is remembered for the "I Have a Dream" speech, but as one *New Yorker* writer put it, the music of the march became the "dream songs" of the Civil Rights era, and in them the Beloved Republic was reborn. Mahalia Jackson, wearing a flowered bonnet belted out "How I Got Over" accompanied by the rolling chords of a church organ. Marian Anderson, introduced "The Whole World in His Hands" in a soft-spoken manner, but her schoolmarm voice turned thunderous when she opened the lower registers to sing, drowning out the sirens of D.C. squealing in the background. Bob Dylan rasped "When the Ship Comes In" while Joan Baez supplied some background harmony. "I'm on My Way," sang Odetta, her voice rising from a kind of rumble beneath the stage skyward like a cry for freedom, and The Freedom Singers rocked the park with the hymn, "I Want My Freedom Now." Peter, Paul and Mary introduced Dylan's "Blowin' in the Wind" and Pete Seeger's "If I Had a Hammer" to the world. An iconic photo of the group from the back shows Mary in white heels and a plain dress flanked by her bearded guitarists in tie and jacket standing before a crowd that stretches beyond the Washington Monument.

But the song that came to symbolize the racial harmony of that march and demonstrated, as Harry Belafonte put it, "that freedom and justice are universal concerns of import to responsible people of all colors," was Joan Baez leading the crowd in "We Shall Overcome." Only twenty-two at the time, she stood alone at the podium in her plaid skirt playing guitar and looking tiny before the throng, but her voice was magnificently commanding, a bell-like peal into the heat of a summer day. The best video of her performance is a partial version of the song in which she does not appear at all. It begins with crowd noise as marchers, black and white, stream onto The Mall, but quickly cuts to the fifth stanza at the line "we are not afraid." The camera zooms out and we get a better sense of the size of the crowd, the screen filled to the edges with milling bodies. When it cuts back to close-ups of small groups, the power of the music to move and unite people becomes palpable. In one frame, a white man with a crew cut and wearing a white shirt stands with several young black men in suits and ties and a young black woman with a ribbon in her hair all singing together. The camera scans forward, each frame containing ten or eleven faces, some in the crowd fanning themselves with flyers to beat back the heat, and every person sings along.

There is majesty in "We Shall Overcome" that can be heard only when it is sung by a group—and the more voices, the greater the impact—so it is in the voices of the crowd that the measure of the moment comes clear. This power reaches full expression in each chorus when the voices rise on the phrase "oh, oh deep," the harmonies opening on the high-pitched long "e" sound, before falling slowly on the words "in my heart." This movement through the harmonic possibilities of a single, mighty chord gives a large gathering of voices room to swell and die together, and at this point in the last chorus in the video, the camera cuts to an engraving at the Lincoln Memorial that begins "in this temple as in the hearts of the people" before the lens descends to the statue of Lincoln himself gazing on the gathering. When the song ends on a few strummed chords, the camera returns to the Washington Monument where the Beloved Republic has been called to order once again.

~ ~ ~

The Beloved Republic wields one weapon: creativity. "The people I admire," Forster wrote, "want to create or discover something." For them, life is not a power grab and certainly not the art of the deal. Instead, they "found religions, great or small, or they produce literature and art, or they do disinterested scientific research." Their creativity may express itself in more ordinary ways like helping others or raising and educating children to be decent human beings. They band together into creative groups such as E. M. Forster's circle of friends at Bloomsbury, the youth mourning for Socrates in the *Apology*, the soirées of scientists meeting at the London home of Joseph Banks, the troubadour poets huddled in fear at Montségur before the advance of murderous crusaders, and the rowdy gang in the Chelsea Hotel in New York. They sing as one in the shadow of the Washington monument and gather at the Orchid Pavilion in ancient China.

Working in mysterious ways, creativity performs wonders. Wang Xizhi studied the sinuous movement in the necks of geese in flight to learn his calligraphic art, a style which he mastered and transformed, and over time he became a figure of legend. In one story he brushed a dot on his stomach every day, thus creating the belly button. In another he turned a pool near the pavilion black from cleaning his brush. A Taoist eager to own one of Wang Xizhi's works of calligraphy and knowing the master's affection for geese, raised a flock of them which he exchanged for a copy of the *Huang Jing Ting*, a famous Taoist meditation, considered the second-finest calligraphic work ever produced, after the *Orchid Pavilion Preface*, of course.

What Wang Xizhi learned from the geese was a flexibility of wrist movement that allowed the lines of his characters to catch the emotion of the moment as his hand moved down the page. The style requires fluidity and grace, more like the movement of a musician's hands than a Western painter's, to achieve the serenity necessary for the art, and as in music a single wrong note or misplaced gesture, can ruin the piece, but also as in music, improvising according to moods is prized, and lines, like blue notes, that move out of the fixed shape can be woven into the larger pattern in a way that only adds to the beauty. It is through this paradoxical mixture of daring and grace that Wang Xizhi was able to draw upon the beauty of his surroundings, the joy of those assembled there, and his own inebriation to create *The Orchid Pavilion Preface*.

The power of such art is ineffable, and when artists and innovative thinkers form a group, they create a heady mix of contraries marked by a fresh way of seeing things. The actual moments of discovery and creativity may have a serene intensity about them like the silence of "a long-legged fly upon the stream," a phrase that the poet William Butler Yeats uses to describe moments of artistic creation and intellectual insight, but the artists themselves are not always serene. Spontaneity, intellectual playfulness, and improvisation born of a generosity of spirit are hallmarks of the Beloved Republic, and many of the artists who wander into this happy congress like a party. Often friendship, aided by intoxicants of various kinds, heats into love or ends in acrimony that frays the edges of the Republic's banner, and ultimately all these various expressions of it come to an end, but the movement itself never goes away and is an on-going affront to the powerful who hope to control or destroy it.

~ ~ ~

Like all that is beautiful the individual creations of the Beloved Republic are vulnerable to destruction. Once the creative spark is kindled, artists gather around the flame to protect, spread, and transform it. They give concerts and readings, refer to each other's works, publish or show or cover each other, form support groups, create MFA programs, return to laboratories late at night, argue in cafés, and gather into movements, but they do not always succeed in protecting the works they produce. Consider the ruins of Palmyra, the slashing of Rembrandt's "Night Watch," the smashing of Michelangelo's "Pietà," or the incalculable losses from the destruction of the library in ancient Alexandria. Pete Seeger was refused record contracts and banned from most concert venues due to his political views. The original copy of the *Orchid Pavilion Preface* was most likely buried along with a Chinese emperor and lost forever.

E. M. Forster knew about the fragility of artworks and of the artists who produce them. He lived in an age of causes, both on the left and on the right, as do we, and realized that imaginative works fostered by friendship could easily be dismissed by dogmatic believers as a "bourgeois luxury." It is hard to create if, as Forster quaintly put it, you get "bonked on the head," especially when the weapon is a spiked mace. It may be true, as the poet and musician Naomi Nye writes, that we "sing ourselves to sleep more than we know," but a song is little protection against starvation, flaming arrows, grenades, drone missiles, and mass deportation forces. When we hear that knock on the door, the singing stops. Brutes take over "sooner or later," Forster admits, and then they "destroy us and all of the lovely things which we have made."

Our only hope during these times, he believes, is to lay low, until those who live by the fist have exhausted themselves. Lay low and help each other. "If I had to choose between betraying my country and betraying my friend," Forster writes, framing the question at the heart of his essay, "I hope I should have the guts to betray my country." The dilemma, let's call it Forster's choice, reveals the challenge to the playful improvisations of art posed by those who are certain that their way is the only way. The Beloved Republic is iconoclastic, allowing its members to smash any truism, cliché, or ideology, thus provoking the ire of the powerful, and stale thinking backed by a fist is a dangerous combination, putting eccentric artists and free-thinking intellectuals in a difficult position. "Probably one will not be asked to make such an agonizing choice," Forster admits, weighing the relative value of friendship and patriotism, but "there lies at the back of every creed something terrible and hard."

In the long run we can be hopeful because these awful periods of human history never last, "for the fortunate reason," Forster explains, perhaps too blithely, "that the strong are stupid." But power does in time give way to beauty. "I realize that society rests upon force," Forster admitted. "But all the great creative actions, all the decent human relations, occur during the intervals when force has not managed to come to the front." During the intervals between these periodic bouts with brutality, the Beloved Republic comes out of hiding, staggers blinking into the light, and begins to create again. Such interludes are "the chief justification for the human experiment," writes Forster, adding, "I call them civilization."

~ ~ ~

In *The Swallows of Kabul* by Yasmina Khadra, a character describes modern Afghanistan under the first rule of the Taliban as a wasteland in which ordinary lives had been robbed of their humanity in the name of God. "We are not anything anymore," she says. "We had some privileges that we didn't know how to defend, and so we forfeited them to the apprentice mullahs." *We had some privileges that we didn't know how to defend*—those words have an ominous echo! In Khadra's novel, the Beloved Republic dwindles down to a frightened couple hiding in shuttered rooms in a Kabul apartment, and eventually the isolation brutalizes them, the helpless feelings they have for one another becoming an instrument of mutual betrayal. I think of the Anne Frank family that came to represent a similar remnant of sensitive and considerate pluckiness rendered helpless in its own country amid the uniformed true believers that Forster decried. And in America I fear we are only one major terrorist strike, emergency decree, or rebellious insurrection away from a collapsed democracy. What happens to the civilized "interval" between wars when we are in perpetual war? Will a song rise? Will it be enough?

Sadly, history offers many examples of unrelenting and horrifying destruction, but one stands out for its violence against art, culture, and love. After a failed crusade in the Arab world at the beginning of the thirteenth century, European Christians turned against themselves in 1209 in a civil war called the Albigensian Crusade. Their targets were Cathar heretics and the troubadour princes who protected them. The troubadours were a largely egalitarian artistic movement that swept through southern Europe during the small renaissance of the twelfth century. Men and women in all classes of society, from the lowly son of an archer to princes and kings, formed groups based solely on artistic ability and created exquisite poetry about impossible love, or *fin' amor*, which they put to song and performed at court. In a world of arranged marriages, these songs were the only place for true romantic emotions to go.

The Catholic Church in Rome resented the troubadours for harboring the heretical Christian Cathars and tried to change the hearts and minds of the free-spirited, humanistic princes of the Occitan region in southern France for decades without success, ultimately resorting to brute force. "Where blessing can accomplish nothing," an exasperated St. Dominic explained to Pope Innocent III, "blows may avail." Many principalities fell during this crusade by Europe against its own people, usually with awful consequences. In the fortified city of Carcassonne, the citizens held out all summer, with troubadours provoking their attackers by singing from the walls, but eventually the water gave out. When the city sued for peace, the prince was imprisoned, and his fifty knights hanged. Later, five hundred citizens were burned alive to prove that the army of God meant business.

The worst massacre occurred in Béziers, another prosperous city near the Mediterranean Sea. The Crusaders demanded that the city give up 222 heretics and the city council proudly refused: "We would rather be drowned in the salt sea than surrender our fellow citizens." The Crusaders broke down the gates and swarmed the city, killing all in their path including seven thousand citizens—women, children, monks, and men—who sought sanctuary in the Church of St. Madeleine cathedral. It was impossible to distinguish between citizens who were heretics and those who were not, so the papal representative, Arnaud Amaury, the Abbot of Citeaux, issued this command: "Kill them all! God will know his own." The order was carried out in a frenzy. After the city fell, Amaury wrote this to Pope Innocent III: "Without regard to age or sex, our forces have put to the sword twenty thousand persons. Divine vengeance works wonders." The infamous

Inquisition had begun, putting a chill on the freedom-loving societies of the Occitan whose citizens cowered under the frowns of true believers in a pattern that would be repeated all too often in Europe and elsewhere.

The last major hold out for the troubadours was the curiously mixed community at Monségur made up of pious Cathar Perfects, warrior knights, noble ladies, common women, and rakish troubadours. Arranged marriages, sanctioned by the Catholic Church, were not recognized in this fortress city, so that the troubadour dream of love based on honest emotions could play itself out in reality. "In Montségur, for the first and last time," the troubadour scholar René Nelli writes, "a society actually practiced and carried to great heights the passionate love of which the troubadours had only worshipped the ideal image under the name of *fin' amor*." Impossible love briefly turned real, and love from afar became love at hand. "These were for the most part truly loving and passionate relationships," Claude Marks writes in *Pilgrims, Heretics, and Lovers*, "for these women had voluntarily accompanied their men into this dangerous predicament and were sharing the hardships and trials."

At Montségur, the Beloved Republic was the glitter of a barbican ablaze in the eyes of a mistress tightening a bandage for her lover. It was a laying on of hands followed by a kiss for a Cathar Perfect undergoing the consolamentum. It was a silk sleeve dragged in the mud. By day large stones tossed from a catapult shook the walls of the citadel as the inhabitants crisscrossed the courtyard attempting to put out fires and defend ramparts. By night men followed hidden passages and secret trails down the mountain to learn news and bring supplies. Men and women, high-born and low-born, their clothes ripped and smeared in blood, struggled together to survive as the flames rose and wooden roofs and timbered walls collapsed, all the while reciting poems and singing songs about the impossible coming true. Here on this rocky outpost, whose name means "mountain of safety," the troubadour movement came to a violent end.

~ ~ ~

Living through a similar moment in history, Forster admitted, "one cannot help getting gloomy and also a bit rattled, and perhaps shortsighted," so his struggle with pessimism during the rise of Hitler is understandable. He knew that the ragtag army of the Beloved Republic could not be victorious over the Nazi enemy, but even though he may have felt helpless, he kept his faith in the nurturing spirit of human beings. "What is good in people," he explains, "and consequently the world," is "their belief in friendship and loyalty for their own sakes" and "their insistence on creation." And during times of war and tyranny, creativity itself is a subversive form of power. "We Will Overcome," a tune sung by poor tobacco workers to help them get through a long day of manual labor became "We Shall Overcome" and instilled in civil-rights leaders like John Lewis and Martin Luther King the courage to transform society. When Mao Zedong and other Communist reformers attempted to eradicate calligraphy in the twentieth century as part of the deadly Cultural Revolution, they failed in part because the legacy of Wang Xizhi's artful characters were over millennia built into the way Chinese people saw the world, and became an intractable, spiritual force against dogma. Even Mao took pride in his bold calligraphy, and the expressiveness of Chinese written characters offers a glimmer of hope as authoritarian rule in China hardens in the twenty-first century. Artists, intellectuals, and scientists can resist by joining movements, taking on causes, or fighting wars of resistance, and many do, but they can also bring about slow but inexorable change by doing what they do best: make art, argue philosophy, teach children, and do the slow, exacting work of science. That is the star that guides them when cruelty seems endless.

The tenacity of the creative spirit, reinforced by benevolence and kindness, is the hidden power of the Beloved Republic. Troubadour princes who sang of *fin' amor* were destroyed by the Crusaders, their palaces usurped, their fortresses ruined, and many of them humiliated and slaughtered, but their songs survived crusades and inquisitions and war to become the poetry of Europe and the basis for romantic love throughout the Western world. They gave us Dante's Beatrice, Petrarch's Laura, *Romeo and Juliet*, the great odes of Keats, and Elizabeth and Mr. Darcy—not to mention an enormous *oeuvre* of Motown songs. The Beloved Republic may at times look moribund, especially in an era ushed in by the likes of Putin and Trump, and I know that the dangers we face now have the potential to be so lethal that we cannot recover from them. But we have faced myriad evils before, and as long as poetry continues to rise unbidden to our lips, and we find feelings to match our words, the civilizing spirit is alive and well, meandering like cups of wine floating down a mountain stream.

THE OTHER STEVE HARVEY

It does only happen on the telephone.

A woman—it is always a woman—and I may be talking about insurance or a credit card or my medications, while I'm standing in the kitchen twirling the telephone cord and the subject of my name comes up. The voice at the other end of the line that had started off business-like, polite, and unaccented, suddenly breaks into a nervous laugh, sheds its formality, and is full of attitude.

It turns black.

"Are you *really* Steve Harvey?"

It happens to those of us with the name of someone who is famous, in my case a black television star known for his charisma, chutzpah, and thick moustache. "I'm here with Steve Harvey," Ellen DeGeneres once joked, "and Steve Harvey's moustache." He is an entertainer who presents himself as saucy, sexy, and full of good cheer.

"I just *love* that man, hmm mm," the voice on the phone once added. "He's *some*thin'."

It is the voice of a black woman letting down her defenses. A woman among friends, and I hear in it an opening, a thinning of the distance between us, even, perhaps, a call to kinship from a confidante, and I usually try to join in with a self-deprecating joke. "No, he's the rich one,"

I say. Or I might be a little evasive. "Me, Steve Harvey? Only on the telephone." Usually, I just tell them what they probably know already: "No, I'm the *other* Steve Harvey."

What I don't say is what I am thinking.

The Other Steve Harvey

I remind people that I had the name first. I was born in Dodge City, Kansas, seven years before the TV star, and my parents chose the name because they liked the sound of it. No one else before me in my family was named Steve as far as I know. My mother called me "Stevie."

As for the name Harvey, my dad's father was a cattle rancher in Dodge City, and the last name has a question mark beside it since that side of the family, unlike my mother's side with a lineage that runs back to a witch in Salem, is not well known. There may be a reason for this blank spot in the record since my dad liked to joke that the Harvey's were probably cattle rustlers and thieves.

Aside from the name, I have little in common with the comedian, Steve Harvey. I was blond when I was young though I am bald now and most of what is left of my hair has turned gray. I live in the north Georgia mountains and for many years taught at Young Harris College, the only source of racial diversity at all in our area at the bottom tip of the Appalachian range, a part of the country long ago settled by Scotch-Irish immigrants after the removal of the Cherokees in the 1830's on the Trail of Tears. When I look at my hands while typing I see that, despite the faded freckles, they are a kind of wheatish-white. Not fish-belly white as Mark

Twain liked to say, but plenty white, and no one who sees me mistakes me for *the* Steve Harvey.

The Other Trayvon Martin

After George Zimmerman, a white neighborhood watch volunteer in Sanford, Florida shot and killed Trayvon Martin, a black high-school student, President Barack Obama responded to a question about the shooting. "If I had a son," he said at a White House press conference, "he would look like Trayvon." After the acquittal of Zimmerman more than a year later, the President, to put the events in context, reiterated the idea more forcibly. "Another way of saying that is Trayvon Martin could have been me thirty-five years ago," he explained, and at the phrase "thirty-five years ago" he shrugged slightly, and a wistful smile briefly crossed his lips, the smile of recognition at a simple truth that had rocked him.

The president said that "there's a lot of pain around what happened here," speaking softly and deliberately though his voice came down hard on the word "pain." Holding it for an extra beat, the word sounded like two syllables, and he extended his cupped hands before him, palms upward, as if they held a great weight before letting them drop down to the lectern again.

"The African American community is looking at this issue through a set of experiences and a history that doesn't go away," he said, pausing, bowing his head and closing his eyes briefly, and, as he gave his examples, I—the other Steve Harvey—began to register some simple truths myself, truths I have known intellectually all of my adult life but had somehow failed to take in as felt experience until I heard the President put them into words.

"There are very few African American men in this country who haven't had the experience of being followed when they were shopping in a department store," the President said looking down at the audience. "That includes me," he added. "There are very few African American men who haven't had the experience of walking across the street and hearing the locks click on the doors of cars. That happens to me, at least before I was a senator." And as he gave this example, he lifted his hand to make the clicking motion with his thumb, and I immediately registered that small gesture as a blow. Yes, I have seen that, I thought leaning in toward the computer screen mesmerized by the president's hands and words. I have *done* that. "There are very few African Americans," the President said finally "who haven't had the experience of getting on an elevator" to find "a woman clutching her purse nervously and holding her breath until she had a chance to get off. That happens often." At the phrase "clutching her purse" the President pulled his hand close to his body reenacting the frightened woman's gesture, becoming her briefly as he remained by reason of his skin color the object of her fear.

That includes me.

That happens to me.

That happens often.

Yes, it does, I admit resignedly, implicated in these scenarios. Steve Harvey and the other Steve Harvey face off across a passenger window, a moustache between them, and I click the lock.

"Where do we take this?" President Obama asked, opening both of his hands outward toward the future, toward all of us, toward me.

He suggested a reexamination of racial profiling practices by police, a review of "stand your ground" laws, and the development of long-term projects to "bolster and reinforce" African American boys, but he also called for "some soul-searching."

He did not look directly into the camera at this moment—he was focused on the reporters sitting in front of him—but he was talking to me, the other Steve Harvey. He asked that Americans be "a little bit more honest" about race and that they at least ask themselves this question: "am I wringing as much bias out of myself as I can?"

As he said those words, he moved his hand three times in a semicircular motion as if twisting a washcloth.

The Other Barack Obama

The facts in the Trayvon Martin shooting are important and in dispute, but, for the purpose of wringing as much bias out of myself as I can, what other people do does not matter. I don't know why Zimmerman was suspicious of an African American teenager walking through his neighborhood wearing a hoodie. I don't know if the words from a dispatcher saying "we do not need you to do that" when he was following Martin in his car was a direct order to stand down. I don't know if Martin broke Zimmerman's nose though it seems amazing to me that we cannot figure that one out. I don't know if racial slurs were exchanged that night.

Did Trayvon Martin say "you are going to die tonight" moments before the shooting as Zimmerman's father said? Or did Zimmerman say that? Like Martin's father I'm pretty suspicious of the detective's claim that Trayvon said "What's your problem, homie?" because they also claim he said "You got me!" when he was shot which sounds like some terrible line from the script of *Gunsmoke*. Was Zimmerman on top of Martin during the scuffle as one witness claimed, pinning him down with his knees or was Martin on top grinding Zimmerman's face into the concrete as another witness said? Or did positions shift during the struggle? And those cries heard in the background of one of the 911 calls—is that Zimmerman screaming or Martin pleading for his life?

I don't know, and I suspect that we will never know for sure, important facts about what happened that evening, but for my purposes here they don't matter. I don't even care what Zimmerman saw when he pulled up in his car beside Trayvon Martin and looked at the young man's face.

What I do care about is what *I* see. What would catch *my* eye on a winter evening in Sanford Florida during rounds of my neighborhood watch when I pull up beside a lone figure and look at the face under a hoodie staring back at me through the passenger window?

And what matters most is what I see first.

The Other?

Even before I lift the hood up over my head, the hoodie feels cozy. When I zip it up, the soft lining wraps around me tighter than a sweater and the pockets go deep in front pulling my shoulders down. In order to drape the hood over me I bow my head a little, and the suggestion of fetal isolation is complete. The mother's other. The only other. The world goes away, and I am ready to wander its empty streets alone.

Well, sort of.

My wife bought the hoodie for me as a Christmas present when I retired from teaching and my children urged me to wear it, going against type. I was always a sweater guy, my favorite an old blue, cotton cardigan with knitted ribbing and tattered cuffs that hangs from a hook in my study. In fact, I knew it was time to retire when I noticed at faculty meetings that I was the only man in the room who wore a cardigan. I would *never* trade one in for a sweatshirt.

But the minute I wrapped myself up in the soft warmth of a hoodie I was a convert. "What was I thinking!" I announced when I lifted the hood over my head and dug my hands into the pockets. "I *love* this!"

Trayvon Martin loved his hoodie too. "It could be a hundred degrees outside, and he always had his hoodie on," his aunt told *USA Today*. The iconic, and controversial, photograph of him that appeared on newscasts and in newspaper reports shows Trayvon in his gray hoodie looking directly at us with soulful eyes and a smooth and youthful skin. The photo is undated leading some to believe that it misrepresents Trayvon as an innocent looking boy though his defense attorney claims it was taken within a year of the shooting.

Was Martin shot because he was a young black man in a hoodie? Many think so. One of the largest rallies after his death was the "Million Hoodie March" at Union Square in Manhattan to protest the racial profiling of non-white youth wearing hoodies. In a photo of the march a crowd gathered to hear Trayvon's father and mother speak, many of them expressing their solidarity with Trayvon as a victim of profiling by draping their hoodies over their heads.

George Zimmerman did not see a person but a hood when he decided to follow Martin in his car; that is the sentiment behind the protest. When he rolled down the window and spoke to Trayvon, he spoke to a dark and hooded face. And when he fired his pistol, he did not shoot Trayvon Martin, a high-school student carrying a bag of Skittles. He shot a hoodie with blackness in it. He shot the other.

The hood isolates. It hides the wearer from the world and invites otherness. Surely this feeling of alienation is why young people wear them as expressions of adolescent rebellion. To be one among a million hoodies—well, more like several thousand—gathered in Union Square, is not to be lost in a crowd, but to be lost to the crowd. The isolation, not the community, gives the wearer a feeling of protection. You can't touch this, the hood says, but the protection is false. Just look at the blood stains and the stippling of powder burns around the bullet holes in Trayvon's hoodie, entered in evidence at the trial.

But there is more to this story of otherness than the hood. Something deeper and intractable. I lift my hoodie from its hanger and put it on, draping the cloth over my head, and walk into the living room to stand before a full-length mirror. Shoving my fists into my pockets I peer into the glass, looking hard at that shaded, freckled face, wondering if I can see the other there.

I can't, but it is not because it is my own face in the mirror.

It is because of what I don't see first. *The* Steve Harvey in my hoodie could be the other, but the other Steve Harvey that I am can't. Anyone who shot me would be aiming at me, not at my hood.

The Mother

Sabrina Fulton, the mother of Trayvon, met with *New York Times* journalist Charles Blow twice to talk about her son's death. In the first interview, conducted at a restaurant near her home five weeks after the shooting, she was accompanied by her mother. "She grows distant when she talks about her loss," Blow wrote, "involuntarily wrapping her hands gently around her mother's arm and resting her head on her mother's shoulder like a young girl in need of comfort. The sorrow seems to come in waves." A year later, in their second interview, she is alone and stronger—her sorrow replaced with a "reservoir of resolve"—but her magical thinking reveals that she is still in mourning. Unable to go to Trayvon's grave, she had begun to collect the gifts given to her in Trayvon's room. "I miss him hugging me," she laments, yearning for no other than her son, and she is puzzled by his death. "I don't know if it's real or not."

The Other Mother

When a pickaninny valentine card fell out of the envelope of a letter that my mother wrote more than fifty years ago, I was surprised. These cards, popular in the fifties, show black children with stereotypical bulging eyes and big, red lips, as well as sexualized body parts that are particularly offensive. I no longer have the postcard, but it looked like one I call up on my computer showing the caricatures of two black children with exaggerated features and coy expressions on their faces standing back-to-back and holding hands. In their free hands the boy clutches a heart and the girl a fan, and in the fingers of their clasped hands there is a note that says, "All about Necking." They look to be about three years old.

My mother died when I was a boy, so I cannot ask her about the valentine, but I was surprised when it tumbled into my lap because I don't remember overtly racist language or symbols from my childhood when she was alive, and I never heard the ugliest racial epithets spoken in my house. My parents used the word "colored" instead, which was common in the fifties, and did so out of politeness or as a refinement preferable to alternatives, I think, unaware that they were labeling another race in a way that could still offend. My parents were moderate Republicans, the party of Lincoln which was, at that time, associated with progressive views on race.

But I suspect, under the surface, an unconscious but pervasive racism was built into my youth, a suspicion that the pickaninny card makes manifest. When my parents shopped for a house in the Northshore area near Chicago, they talked openly to each other about housing values and race. They chose Deerfield which Harry and David Rosen called "The Little Rock of the North" in their book *But Not Next Door*, the town becoming notorious in 1959 when a developer attempted unsuccessfully to build integrated housing units there. In a letter my mother, aware of the controversy, was relieved that the residents of Deerfield blocked the project by voting "to build several park areas" in disputed neighborhoods of the town. "Deerfield is truly a town of nice, wholesome people," she wrote, the words "nice" and "wholesome" covering over a host of unspoken sins.

I think if my mother were alive today and in an elevator when *the* Steve Harvey walked in, she would clutch her purse nervously and hold her breath until she had a chance to get off.

The Other Father

In his speech, President Obama said that "things are getting better." "Each successive generation," he explained, chopping the air above the podium into segments with his hand, "seems to be making progress in changing attitudes when it comes to race." Gesturing toward the family residence in the East Wing, he mentioned his daughters as examples: "When I talk to Malia and Sasha, and I listen to their friends, and I see them interact." Here the President paused, composing his thoughts: "they're better than we are—they're better than we were—on these issues." He admitted that America was not "post-racial," and that racism had not been "eliminated," and that we needed to work on these challenges. He said that leaders needed to "encourage the better angels of our nature" rather than use episodes like the shooting of Trayvon Martin "to heighten divisions," and he paused after the word "divisions" for a full four seconds, looking off into the middle distance, before returning to the optimism his children represent to him. "But we should also have confidence that kids these days, I think, have more sense than we did back then, and certainly more than our parents did, or our grandparents did; and that along this long, difficult journey, we're becoming a more perfect union—not a perfect union, but a more perfect union."

The Other

When I pull off at the Tenth Street exit in downtown Atlanta and a handful of black men rush at the car armed with Windex bottles and washcloths as a scam to get money, I click the lock on my door. When I drive through the inner city to visit my daughter, I click the lock on my door. When I walk into downtown neighborhoods, I move my wallet to my front pocket. When I go to a Braves' game at Turner Field, I walk behind my family to keep an eye on them. I don't tell racist jokes, and at a party when someone does, I don't laugh or acknowledge the ugly word, but I do remain silent.

And as I make these admissions to myself and vow after the President's speech to do better, I picture in my mind a hand turning slowly as if wringing a washcloth.

Then suddenly it stops.

Many years ago, I was at the house of my friend, John Kneiss, in the mountains where I live, admiring a framed photograph he had taken of black children at a playground. The kids were scrambling to get into the shot, their faces alive with mischievous delight, especially one of the girls in a white dress who clearly had elbowed her way to get her big smile in front of the camera.

"Racism will be with us," my friend said, nodding toward the picture, "as long as the first thing you notice about these children is that they are black."

I turned and looked hard at the picture again. When I had looked at it before I had registered delight, playfulness, mischievousness, and spunkiness, but the first thing I saw was that their faces were black.

I think my friend is right.

It is prejudice, this *first* thing I see, a judgement based on race before any other facts are known. President Obama asked us—asked *me*— to be a "bit more honest." Well, if I met Barack Obama on the street, a man I voted for twice to be President, I'm pretty sure the first thing I would in all honesty see is that he is black.

Another Trayvon

So what do I see when I look at the face of Trayvon Martin under his hoodie? In reverse order, I see the smoothness of his skin. I keep coming back to that. He really is just so damned young under that gray hoodie, a kid and nothing more.

And he really could be Barack Obama thirty-five years ago. I see that in the wounded innocence of his seventeen-year-old face, the hint of mischief in his smile, and a dreaminess about the eyes.

I could see menace here, too, a twisting of these features in anger that could be a threat, but in repose it is a face that a mother, a girlfriend, or a father would love.

I see his black hair forming a kind of crown around the face, framing it, containing it.

The pupils of his eyes, highlighted with flecks of light, are otherwise black and penetrating. They float dolefully from the upper eyelids in the eggshell white of his eyes. And the eyebrows rise, almost elfin.

His nose has a small hump in the middle and a hint of a moustache appears above his upper lip.

His skin is buttery brown and there is something feminine about its smoothness, inviting the touch.

But the first thing I see when I look at the face of Trayvon Martin as I imagine him bending down to speak to me through the window of my car on a cool winter night in Sanford, Florida, is not the buttery brown skin, the suggestion of a moustache, or the doleful eyes under the hoodie.

The first thing I see is that he is black.

And what I see first is what I think first.

The Other Steve Harvey

So, I tell my Steve Harvey jokes. "He's the rich one," I say. Or "I had the name before he did." Or "only on the telephone." What I don't say is the first thing that comes to my mind when anyone asks me if I'm really Steve Harvey. "No, he's the black one." Under the hoodie of my silence, that thought floats into my mind first, revealing an unconscious bias I cannot wring out of myself. When I tell the jokes, being self-deprecatory, of course, to disarm the situation, I drive my prejudice down in me where it is not apparent but does not die.

"Where do we take this?" President Obama asked, opening both of his hands outward toward the future, toward all of us, toward me. If I am an employer, it takes me to a tendency to say no too quickly, and if a juror to say guilty too easily, and if a cop to shoot before a threat is real. When I judge the death of Trayvon Martin and other black men killed by authorities under mysterious circumstances, it takes me to a conclusion contrary to all I have been taught: that the burden of proof is on the shooter. Most of all it takes me to what I see first. When I see a black man, I must teach myself to see a father, husband, or son. When I see a black woman, I must teach myself to see a sister and a potential friend. But it won't be easy to change what I see and think first. Every time I tell the joke about my name, a pickaninny valentine card tumbles from the fingertips of memory, and I'm secretly clicking the lock on my car door. I'm surreptitiously checking my wallet in the elevator. I'm following Steve Harvey through the aisles of a department store, watching his hands.

Madre Luz

On a misty Monday afternoon a few days after the violent protests in Charlottesville, artist Pablo Machioli patched up and painted the toppled statue of Madre Luz. With the help of friends, he lifted the papier-mâché installation into position in front of the statue of Stonewall Jackson and Robert E. Lee in Baltimore's Wyman Park. Madre Luz is larger than life and naked from the waist up requiring four men to hold her in their arms and embrace her to tilt her upright. In her vulnerability she draws people to her that way and asks them to become their better selves. Some listen, and the battering she took from those who do not make her look even more majestic: a chipped statue of a pregnant black woman carrying a child in a brightly-colored sling on her back. Originally Madre Luz had been facing away from Jackson and Lee, but this time, sensing her command of the moment, the men slowly turned her doleful face and raised golden fist toward her oppressors.

Decades ago, when my wife and I lived a few blocks from Wyman Park, we often passed by the double equestrian statue of the Lee-Jackson Monument that loomed over one of the entrances. I hardly gave it a thought. I was in graduate school at the time, and Barbara, my wife, worked at Johns Hopkins in the admissions office. We spent most of our free-time before we had kids deep in conversations about art, poetry, ideas, and our future. We loved the city, especially that park, where many in the neighborhood would gather for lunches and watch dogs chase Frisbees.

Rarely did the statue catch my eye, and I certainly knew nothing of its history.

Barbara says that she did notice how beautiful the horses were, and looking at photos of the two mounted confederates now, I see it. The horses are stunningly rendered. Lee's steed has come to a stop, both feet planted, and gazes down, forelock draped over the bridle strap and ears perked, alert. Jackson is pulling back on the reins of his horse, but the animal resists, its mouth drawn taut by the bridle and nostrils flared, with one leg held mid-air and chest muscles flexed. It is the eyes of Jackson's horse, a wide-eyed fear captured in bronze, that is arresting. It is afraid of you, you realize, if you stand before it and gaze up, making you a part of the artwork, and for a few days the raised fist of Madre Luz filled that horse with a terror that caused Jackson and Lee, and all they represent, to retreat.

~ ~ ~

On the base of the Lee-Jackson Monument someone spray-painted "REMEMBER C-VILLE" in crude letters. Lately I have been having a hard time not remembering Charlottesville, another place where I lived and went to school. It is hard to erase the faces of more than one hundred men carrying torches across The Lawn at UVA and snaking through the Grounds to the statue of Thomas Jefferson, making animal sounds and chanting "blood and soil" and "you will not replace us" and "Jews will not replace us." The organizers clearly wanted to re-enact marches by Nazi youth in Germany before World War II, evoking feelings of disgust in those who watched by shocking us, and they succeeded.

"I'm carrying a pistol. I go to the gym all the time. I'm trying to make myself more capable of violence," said the racist Christopher

Cantwell in an interview with Elle Reeve of VICE News before the march to the Robert E. Lee statue in Emancipation Park. That's a shocker. Here's another. "I'm here to spread ideas, talk in the hopes that somebody more capable will come along and do that, someone like Donald Trump who does not give his daughter to a *Jew*." Cantwell spits out the word "Jew" with a smirk on his face to the muted laughter of young men behind him. "I don't think you could feel about race the way I do and watch that Kushner bastard walk around with that beautiful girl, okay?" The language is sexually charged on purpose. Reeve is a petite blonde reporter and Cantwell attempts to show off by provoking her—at times it looks and sounds like verbal abuse as she struggles successfully to maintain her poker face.

Sadly, there's more and it gets worse.

"This city is run by Jewish communists and criminal niggers," said Robert Ray, another neo-Nazi. He goes by the name Azzmador and writes for *The Daily Stormer*, a magazine which promotes racist ideas and trolls its critics in an ugly and mean-spirited way. To him words are weapons and he is fond of using imagery of infestation to attack. "We're showing to this parasitic class of anti-white vermin that this is our country, this country was built by our forefathers," he explains in a manner that is creepily measured given his words, but as he talks his voice rises as if he's giving a speech, and turns strident. He calls his enemies "antiwhite, anti-American filth," bearing down hard on the word "filth" for dramatic effect, and shouts that at some point Neo-Nazis "will have enough power that we will clear them from the streets forever," an unmistakable nod toward ethnic cleansing and the mass deportations and extermination of Jews and others during the Nazi era. "That which is degenerate in white countries," Ray eventually yells, "will be removed."

It is a verbal cesspool, all of it. So, yes, after watching those images and hearing all of that word bilge, I have no trouble remembering C-ville. I can't get it out of my mind.

~ ~ ~

Neo-Nazis are defined by what they are most proud of and the list is ugly. Cantwell likes to parade around half naked showing off his torso. Throughout much of the VICE News film he protests with his shirt off, although in fairness he may have done that because he was maced and had to wash his head and neck with milk. He and his fellow protestors are proud of creating a tangible, as opposed to an online, spectacle. "They're supposedly here to protest the removal of a statue of Robert E. Lee," Reeve explains, "but they're really here to show that they are more than an internet meme, that they're a big, real presence that can organize in physical space." So, biceps and pecs and abs and helmets and shields and tear gas. Size matters, too. "They have a lot of numbers," Reeve reports, and Robert Ray, who sports a scraggily gray beard, glasses, and a ballcap—and fortunately kept his tee-shirt on—brags about the turnout when he says "we greatly outnumbered" the counter-protesters. "Last night at the torch walk there were hundreds and hundreds of us," he explains. "People realize that they are not atomized individuals. They are part of a larger whole."

They are also proud of their name calling. It is not just the meaning of the words, dehumanizing banalities such as "vermin" and "filth" with Nazi associations, but the way they deliver these insults for effect. Ray may be listing his insults with the demeaner of an accountant tallying up tax liabilities, but when he raises his voice, there is something wooden about his delivery that belies the real motive of his performance, the calculated attempt to use words to intimidate. More natural in his delivery, Cantwell is particularly adept at twisting his face around insults and shoving them at Reeve, but it is still clear that it is all for effect. In fact, he has a knack, which he shares with Trump, of making all language sound insulting, each word weaponized. When he says "we're here obeying the law, we're doing everything we're supposed to do, trying to express opinions," the words are innocuous enough in themselves and we get the point, but we also hear in the menacing delivery that the words express more than opinions. They are vehicles of hatred. All of them. Spitbombs. Verbal gunshots.

It is not an accident that Cantwell mimics Trump talk. Neo-Nazi's are proud of their association with the President, another fact that defines them. Cantwell may lament that the President would "give his daughter to a Jew," but he punctuates the slur with a Trump-like hand gesture using his forefinger and thumb. Trump equates neo-Nazi's with other protesters by blaming "many sides" for violence in the Charlottesville protests and asking rhetorical questions about the "alt-left" attacking the "alt-right," and this implicit support now and during his campaign has already had an effect, emboldening these groups to stage events like Charlottesville. In a tweet, David Duke, the former Grand Wizard of the Klan, thanked Trump for having the "courage to tell the truth." The neo-Nazis are a fringe group now, and the 300,000 subscribers to *The Daily Stormer* make up only a fraction of Trump's base. At most white nationalist rallies they are outnumbered by counter-protesters, but the President's subtle endorsement boosts their ranks. If Charlottesville is a harbinger, that number sadly will grow.

~ ~ ~

Madre Luz faces this swelling odiousness and raises a golden fist.

Pablo Machioli, an artist from Uruguay who has lived in Baltimore since 2003 designed Madre Luz to "create a conversation" about race. The name means "mother light," but in Spanish it is associated with "dar a luz," a phrase referring to giving birth and nurturing life. In an interview with *Baltimore Sun* reporter Christina Tkacik, the artist explained that his original idea was to construct a statue of Harriet Tubman throwing a brick, but he rejected that as too violent and chose instead a pregnant mother as a symbol of life. "I feel like people would understand and respect that," he told the reporter, but standing defiantly in front of the Lee-Jackson monument, I believe she symbolizes more because her imposing presence combines maternal nurturing with power. Madre Luz is Gaia, The Triple Goddess, and The Mother's Knot. She is the American Statue of Maternity. She is the African seed of the wawa tree. She is a black flame.

What strikes me most is the majestic power of her nakedness. She wears a white skirt with the upper half of her ebony body fully exposed. The pregnant belly and breasts droop heavily but the sling on her back carrying a child seems to pull her upright, standing triumphant despite the burden of life here and to come weighing her down. Her left arm is broken and repaired in two places but still upright. Her nearly featureless face bears a doleful but stoic expression, and the scratches and rips in the papier-mâché only add to her fearlessness. There is defiance in the pose, but the roundness of her body and the widening s-shaped curve of her fully erect self is invitation as well, a summons to do your best or do your worst. She has been embraced, photographed, and admired. She has been beaten, toppled, and thrown to the ground only to rise again. She has heard it all— all the bile of Cantwell and Ray and the other racists—and she can stand before their symbol of white supremacy, powerless and exposed, and still raise a fist sprinkled with glitter.

Her nakedness defies the violence it invites.

~ ~ ~

Violence is, in the end, what the neo-Nazis want. "I came pretty well prepared for this thing today," Cantwell tells Reeve in his motel room in Roanoke Rapids, N.C. as he raises an AK assault rifle and tosses it on the bed. Next, he pulls a pistol from under his belt. "KelTec P3AT," he says, tossing it on the mattress beside his rifle. He offers up that addled half-smile of his. He loves this. "GLOCK 19, nine-millimeter." He lifts the gun from behind his back and, sighting down the barrel briefly tosses it on the bed. He raises his pantleg and undoes the Velcro holster on his calf. "Ruger LC9, also nine-millimeter." He's doing a lethal-weapon striptease for Reeve. "And there's a knife." He finds it in his side pocket and flips it. "Oh," he says as an afterthought, "I actually have another AK in that bag over there." Divested of his weapons he turns to Reeve. "You can lose track of your fucking guns, huh."

Cantwell tossing the weapons is visual assault.

Reeve, still poker-faced but with her chin puckered, looks like a victim.

The bed looks like a crime scene.

Cantwell believes that his band of white nationalists exhibited self-control during the demonstrations. He thought that the death of Heather Heyer was justified claiming that the crowd of counter-protesters James Alex Fields plowed into with his car provoked the death by "striking" the car. "When these animals attacked him again, he saw no way to get away from them except to hit the gas," Cantwell explained, describing the video of the death scene as he saw it. "The amount of restraint that our people showed out there I think was astounding," he added sternly, but unconvincingly.

We can all watch the video. It is hard to see the Dodge Challenger accelerating into a milling crowd without braking and not call it murder. It's hard to watch the car back up, accelerating again, as bodies flip over the trunk or slide under the back bumper and not call it terrorism. It's impossible to listen to Cantwell talk calmly beside a bed full of weapons and not fear that these white nationalists call anything but all-out war restraint. "We're *not* non-violent: we'll fucking *kill* these people if we have to," Cantwell yelled at one point, adding, bluntly, that "more will die." He means it. He wants it. He is prepared to do it. He wants the masked Antifa, the small number of counter-protesters who believe in physical resistance to the neo-Nazis, to strike with their sticks and flagpoles, provoking a race war, a war he thinks he can win. That's what the guns on the white bedspread are all about. The weapon of choice this time may have been a car with a detached bumper pulling away pathetically from murder and mayhem, but these guys are just itching to use their personal arsenals.

What stands in their way is the naked body of Madre Luz.

~　~　~

"I don't think it's ever been about a statue," said Tanesha Hudson, a local activist from Charlottesville who spoke to a reporter from VICE News. It is true that as a black woman she puts up with the oppressive presence of Confederate statues daily. She "can't stand in one corner" of her city and not feel "the master" staring down on her, she admits. But the call to take down the statue of Robert E. Lee was not what brought the white nationalists to her city. That was an excuse for a show of force and a display of hatred intended to provoke a face-off, and, in the end, the question is, not what the white nationalists do, but the way others in this confrontation respond.

"It's about right is right and wrong is wrong," Hudson explained, her assertion of morality a challenge. With bigotry on one side, who are we on the other and how will we fight back?

The question is "What will I do with my anger and disgust?"

The answer is not throw a brick.

~ ~ ~

I try hard to hear respect for the law when David Duke explains that his people had "a federal court order to have this rally" as he left Emancipation Park. I would like to muster up some sympathy for Ray when he talks about young, white men feeling lost, atomized, and alone in America. I would certainly like to know what kind of insecurity causes Cantwell to say hateful things and then search Reeve's face, which is the face of us all, for signs of shock. But I can't. All of that talk was an excuse to create an explosive, and ultimately violent, spectacle for Americans to witness on their screens. The old guard of neo-Nazis and the KKK who talk like Cantwell and Ray is probably a lost cause, a pathetic group who actually are deplorable.

Even the younger men whose post-adolescent minds are still forming and susceptible to other messages, seem like lost causes. The chant of "you will not replace us" as they march across the Virginia campus may offer up an unspoken message of white anxiety about having *no* place in a changing world that will *dis*-place them, and as they approach the counter-protesters who link arms and form a ring around the base of the statue of Thomas Jefferson, the youthful physicality and camaraderie of both groups looks about the same, but the fury of the neo-Nazis is palpable, the voices reverberating in my mind like the ringing after a blow even now. I can't hear a cry for help no matter how hard I try in the words they spit out. I hear nothing but racism. How can we stop this contagion of hatred from spreading?

The ones who concern me are the millions of young people who are watching it from the sidelines on social media. They are susceptible to hate-speech and propaganda and follow trends, but they are also ripe for change when a more mature self emerges, one capable of empathy, of re-placing themselves in the shoes of others before they speak and act. They do not need a violent face-off that begins with sticks, rocks, and mace and ends in gunfire. They need to see real courage in the form of a non-violent response the way I did when I was a kid and was changed for life by the civil rights protests I saw on television. They need moral leadership to awaken their consciences before it is too late, someone exposed and vulnerable who can speak to their better selves.

They need a fist of gold to lead them out of this torchlit hell.

~ ~ ~

A crane lifted the enormous double equestrian statue from its pedestal in the pre-dawn dark. A hard hat with a local construction crew guided it using rope under the glare of trailer-mounted lights as Madre Luz calmly watched. Around the city of Baltimore other controversial Confederate statues were pulled down that day, loaded onto flatbed trucks, and taken to a municipal parking lot. There Lee and Jackson and their beautiful horses stood in an unfamiliar spot, looking a little forlorn, among statues of confederate women, a dying soldier, a winged angel, and a robed figure slumped beside the hedges.

For two days after the removal of the Lee-Jackson Monument, Madre Luz stood triumphant, representing the only way to fight hatred: allowing vulnerability to penetrate the consciousness, and prick the consciences, of Americans. It worked at the Edmund Pettus Bridge when Martin Luther King, John Lewis, Jesse Douglas, James Forman, and Ralph Abernathy locked arms and marched toward Selma. It worked at a segregated lunch counter in Jackson, Mississippi when college students staged a sit-in. It happened in Charlottesville when Heather Heyer's mother, Susan Bro, stood defiantly at her daughter's funeral and announced, magnificent in her grief, that white nationalists "tried to kill my child to shut her up, but guess what, you just magnified her." And it was on full display as Madre Luz, a symbol of maternal love and justice, stood before a Rebel statue and watched it being hauled away. The reward of passive resistance is increased awareness, and I think back on the many times Barbara and I walked past the Lee-Jackson monument oblivious to the burden it placed on the city. Now we know. Peaceful protestors force us to confront truths beyond ourselves and see past our blindness.

Often they pay a price. Susan Bro lost her daughter. John Lewis and others were beaten when state and local police at the bridge near Selma attacked marchers with billy clubs and tear gas. The lunch-counter protesters were humiliated as white townspeople swarmed around them and poured sugar, ketchup, and mustard over their heads.

And Madre Luz was in the end destroyed. To celebrate her moment of triumph the artist moved her to the pedestal where the equestrian statues had stood for sixty-nine years, but in the middle of the night someone knocked her over, breaking her body in several pieces as it fell headlong. The price for nonviolence is high, but it is an answer to hatred that produces results. After the Civil War, any durable gains of the movement for civil rights in America have largely been achieved by courageous, nonviolent protest, and if the movement turns violent, the bigots win. The way out of hatred is to follow Madre Luz. Mother Light. In the end, her upper torso was crushed and her head smashed in, but her golden fist remains intact reaching out of the ruin to us all.

One Boy's Luminous Skin

It is butter. The sun's pillow. The moon's snow. His eyes with large brown irises are a woodsy invitation to a boy's life. They glitter with a hint of mischief too, but I'm talking about skin.

One boy's luminous skin.

His teeth are a little goofy with two adult front teeth and some baby teeth in the back, but I'm not talking about them either. A cowlick sends his hair awry—and that matters because my grandson has a cowlick in the same spot—but I won't be diverted here.

Consider one boy's luminous skin,

smoothed from light by a sculptor, ready for a grandfather's thumb to wipe off tears or stains or blood.

One boy's skin,

the tough epidermis, the dermis webbed with nerves made for pain, and the subcutis gloppy with glands and arteries and veins and blood—so much blood.

One boy's luminous skin

blooming where the bullet enters, turning to jelly, and closing back in on itself with a hiss, and the lung blooming with a hiss and the heart blooming with a hiss and the bullet blooming blood where the hot hiss exits

one boy's luminous

filleted open, scalpel following hiss in the dark, retractor spreading ribs, glove messaging heart, and blood, so much blood, blood everywhere.

Luminous. Liminal. Lost.

If he does not look like your grandson, then maybe this girl with chestnut hair in a different photo is yours. Or this boy with red hair and—my God!—that gap for his two front teeth. Do any of you have a granddaughter with a smile as wide and dimpled as the one in this photo? What about this one or that one or—oh no, look at those bright eyes.

Luminous. Lusterless. Lost.

I'm leaving out names. I don't want to add to the misery. I'm leaving out names for you to fill in one of your own,

one luminous

child with brown eyes or green eyes or hazel or cobalt or robin's-egg blue

eyes—can you find your color there? This child age six, that child age six,

or this one, that one, or this one, age *six*. Hell, we were *all* age six once!

Consider one boy's luminous skin

and blood, so much blood, blood on us all.

THE ARC OF THE UNIVERSE

Outside the Art Glass studio, Lake Chatuge lies serene, like a languid lover among the blanket folds of the southern Appalachian Mountains, while inside the chaos of creation roars. David Goldhagen has just pulled red-hot glass out of the glowing glory hole beside his furnace and is slowly opening the ball by swirling the molten bubble at the tip of the punty. My daughter, Alice, and her partner, Namrata, two beautiful, young women radiant with love for one another watch front and center while my wife and I stand nearby, all of our eyes flickering. Donald Trump has been elected President, and the 24/7 news station behind the glass artist blares left-wing spin from the radio, the hosts joking about proper birthday gifts for Speaker of the House, Paul Ryan, who capitulated on the newly-installed President's Muslim Travel Ban.

"We should get him a spine and a soul," the announcer says, reading a listener's tweet, "and look at *this*," he adds with a laugh. Someone has changed the Wikipedia entry for invertebrates to include a photo of Paul Ryan "in with the jellyfish, velvet worms, and spiders."

At least I think that's what he says. It's hard to hear a radio over the bellowing furnace.

David, a long-time liberal, looking disheveled and happy, floats among his droning machines like a sea creature. Lifting the ball of red hot, molten glass high above his head to check the shape, he shouts over the blast that he has a present for The Speaker too. "If he walked through that door, I'd toss this to him and say catch."

In my mind I see the fiery globe sail like a meteor across the studio.

~ ~ ~

I don't remember where my wife and I began the conversation we needed to have. We may have been in bed, just after turning off the light, my wife in the crook of my arm for a moment of quiet talk.

"Yes, but they love each other," I said into the dark.

Or maybe I waited until we had already pulled the sheet and blanket over our shoulders, settled our pillows, and turned away from each other to sleep.

Maybe we were in the den where we always have our morning talks while sitting on the sofa drinking coffee, the sun pouring through the winter plants and glass balls hanging in the recess of the bow window.

Or along the path that dips down to Lake Nottely and winds through the woods of Meeks Park where we take our afternoon walks, thinking, talking it out, thinking, changing our minds.

"I'm just glad they're happy," you said.

Knowing us, we had the conversation over and over for months. Weeding the tendrils of dodder from the ivy bed. Watering the fiddlehead fern in the front yard. Negotiating the glittering trajectory of water from the sprinkler in the side yard, getting the coverage just right. Wills inexorably bending.

Or maybe it *was* in David's shop. "I'm glad they can be together openly," I said, when we separated ourselves from the girls to choose the engagement gift and your hands fell on a rainbow swirl of glass, holding the gift out with both hands as if testing the weight, raising an eyebrow.

~ ~ ~

But is an arched eyebrow enough? "Like a drawn bow," writes Lao Tzu, "the moral universe brings high and low together," implying that the arc of the universe becomes moral by itself, forgetting that drawing the bow requires proper comportment. The archer should not "blerith out his tongue," "byteth his lips" or "holdeth his neck awrye," writes "Old Toxophilus" in his 1833 commentary on "The Five Points of Archery" by Roger Ascham written in 1545. He should avoid "wrychinge with his back" as though someone had pinched his "behinde." He definitely should not lean back and "layeth out his buttocks" as if afraid of the target and above all should not run behind the arrow "dancinge and hoppinge after his shaft as it flyeth."

Instead he should draw the bow by "coming round," bringing it as close as possible to an O-shape, which is not a mere matter of strength, but a "method that will affect what force cannot." The release of the arrow should be one motion accomplished by instinct rather than thought or control, a "loosing *while* drawing, without making any pause." In practice, the old teacher admitted resignedly, the best archers often "paused for a moment and corrected their aim" before releasing the shaft, but this holding should be "the briefest of pauses so as not to put too much strain on the bow."

"It must occupy so little time, that it may be perceived better in the mind when it is done, than seen with the eye when doing."

Do disguised as don't.

Lao Tzu would have approved.

~ ~ ~

Theodore Parker was less sure, though he too was drawn to supple metaphors for the way the universe works. On a Sunday in 1852 high and low gathered to hear his sermon on the subject "Of Justice and Conscience" on the stage of the Melodeon in Boston. "Turn and do Justice," the abolitionist that some dismissed as a heretic began, reading from the apocryphal *Book of Tobias* in a building which served as a music hall during the week.

He was anxious that the moral universe is less reliable than the physical one. The "law of right," is mighty, a "river of God that is full of blessing" bringing justice to the world in a torrent, he announced standing in his customary black broadcloth among the spangles of dancers from the night before. But "it does not work free from all hindrance." Having "private nutations, oscillations, and aberrations, personal or national," the will of people, he complained, "may conflict for a time" with the trajectory of justice.

He was thinking of human beings in chains.

His faith told him that "the ploughshare of justice is drawn through and through the field of the world, uprooting savage plants," and will in the end be victorious, but he had heard the whirling whip crack across black backs and saw no end to slavery.

"I do not pretend to understand the moral universe," he admitted, "the arc is long, my eye reaches but little ways." He "cannot calculate the curve" or extrapolate its full shape, and what glows like a falling star in his conscience grows dim in a real world of auction blocks, shackles, and nooses tossed across a limb, but "from what I see," he assured his congregation, "it bends toward justice."

~ ~ ~

Following the arc of justice to Príncipe Island off the coast of West Africa on April 29, 1919, Englishman Arthur Eddington nearly missed seeing the eclipse that would change our understanding of the universe forever. He was too busy fiddling with his instruments: changing plates on the astrograph and adjusting the mirrors of aging coelostats. "I did not see the eclipse," he wrote later, "except for one glance to make sure it had begun, and another half-way through to see how much cloud there was." He worried that an early morning storm might ruin his work.

His immediate goal was to confirm Albert Einstein's General Theory of Relativity by showing that the gravity of the sun bent light coming from distant stars, a deflection that can be measured during a total eclipse, but he also had justice on his mind, and another goal of the experiment, just as important in his eyes, was moral: to return a spirit of internationalism to the sciences after World War I and dispel the wartime view of many British and American scientists that some depravity of character tainted all discoveries made by Germans.

Eddington, a Quaker and a conscientious objector, desired, in Einstein's words, to "throw a bridge over the abyss of misunderstanding" by confirming the theories of a theoretical physicist from Germany. So, he stood in a waterproof hut on a beach in Africa taking photographs and gathering data as the cloudy sky slowly cleared. If he got a break in the weather and his jittery equipment held up, he hoped to forge the arc of starlight bent like a scimitar around the sun into an instrument of peace.

~ ~ ~

"How long?" Martin Luther King Jr. asked as he stood under the dome of the state capital in Montgomery, Alabama, on March 25, 1965 after successfully completing the march from Selma. "Not long!" he declared, answering his own question. Nonviolence "can transform dark yesterdays into bright tomorrows. No lie can live forever."

"How long?" he asked again, his voice a trumpet summoning the crowd. "Not long," he answered, "because you shall reap what you sow."

"Yes sir," the crowd murmured, and "No sir" and "speak, speak, speak," as a call and response began.

"How long?" King asked again. "Not long," he insisted, "because the arc of the moral universe is long, but it bends toward justice."

There is hope and confidence in his voice as he echoes the words of Theodore Parker and exuberant delight on the faces of others on the stage, an invisible halo forming above the whole scene, but the man himself never smiles and the pictures his words conjure up in the mind tell a different story. Justice is wounded and "lying prostrate on the streets of Selma and Birmingham and communities all over the South," and a blinding prejudice drives "bright-eyed wisdom from her sacred throne." Hope may be "a radiant star," but it has yet to be "plunged against the nocturnal bosom of this lonely night." And where does that hope for a just world come from? Where does the drooping bough of the moral universe begin? It is rooted in slavery and "plucked from weary souls with chains of fear and the manacles of death." Justice is "crucified," the moment is "difficult," and the hour "frustrating."

The future "sways" like a hangman's noose.

The arc of the moral universe may bend toward justice as King declared, but it is long.

How long?

Truth is "forever on the scaffold," he intoned, and wrong is "forever on the thrown" and forever is a long, long time.

~ ~ ~

"Why don't you guys do something," a lesbian shouted to a crowd of gay onlookers who were milling about. She had been "roughed up" in the Stonewall bar according to historian David Carter in the film *Stonewall: Profiles in Pride*, and scuffled with police who dragged her to a patrol wagon. Her name was probably Stormé DeLarverie, a butch cross-dresser, though no one knows for sure.

"And then everything went crazy," says Martin Boyce who is identified as a "Stonewall Rebellion Veteran" in the film. It happened on a Friday night, June 27, 1969, during a police raid on the bar. The patrons resisted, saying "don't touch me," "get your hands off me," and "I have my civil rights, too." As the police began arresting people, trying to move them out of the bar, the crowd outside swelled and began unexpectedly pushing back, throwing bottles and stones. "The police were stunned," explains Jerry Hoose, who is also identified as a veteran of Stonewall. Eventually for their own safety the cops retreated into the building and called for reinforcements.

"The scene which I will never forget" says Hoose, were "all the drag queens" who locked arms to do "a Rockettes kickline." Dancing to the tune of "Ta-ra-ra Boom-de-ay," they sang "We are the Stonewall Girls/ We wear our hair in curls." When Hoose looks up, uncertain of the next line, Boyce finishes the stanza, "We wear our dungarees/ Above our nelly knees/ When it comes to boys/ We merely hypnotoize."

"That was enough for them," says Boyce. Police in riot gear attacked the line of unarmed and defenseless queens with billy clubs. "The cops just got us."

~ ~ ~

Barbara and I were not a hard sell. We were in Ecuador where Alice served in the Peace Corps and Barbara thinks that we were walking along the festive Malacon in Guayaquil. "I like men," Alice said, "but I also like women." It was a hard time for her. Riding buses in rocky, mountainous terrain seriously damaged her back, and she was lonely and sexually confused.

For us it was no surprise. We had our suspicions and, of course, were supportive as she talked, her head bent forward and her brown hair falling on both sides of her cheeks, but there is a difference between saying the right things, believing the right things, and feeling them. She had already had some broken relationships, and Barbara was worried that being gay would only add to her burdens. For me, there was also a difference between having lifelong gay friends and knowing your own daughter is gay, and I was uncertain what all that meant about her future and ours. Her past and ours. For several years we worried about her even after she came home, recovered slowly from her back injuries, went to graduate school, and found a job as a dual-language counselor.

Eventually, it came to this: all we wanted was for her to be happy.

Like a looping vine, the arc unwinds.

~ ~ ~

"The whole atmosphere of tense interest was exactly like that of Greek drama," wrote the philosopher Alfred North Whitehead when Arthur Eddington and his team of scientists stood beneath the portrait of Isaac Newton and presented their findings on the 1919 eclipse to the Royal Society in London. Since the deflection of starlight as it passed near the sun was larger than predicted by conventional physics, Eddington insisted that Einstein's law of gravitation had replaced Newton's law.

"Revolution in science," declared the London *Times*. "New Theory of the Universe" and "Newtonian Ideas Overthrown." *The Illustrated London News* devoted a full page of drawings of the observation station including a map and several views of the eclipse to illustrate the amount of deflection under the caption, "Starlight Bent by the Sun's Attraction."

In an article promoting the experiment, Eddington wrote that the work of Albert Einstein enriched our understanding of the natural world in a way "comparable with, or perhaps exceeding the advances associated with Copernicus, Newton and Darwin."

Albert Einstein "of Berlin."

The president of the Royal Society called it "one of the highest achievements in human thought." Einstein taught us that the solar system twists on itself like a "gigantic, flexible snail shell" the astronomer Carlo Rovelli wrote later, and planets drop into its wide opening like "a marble that rolls in a funnel," falling into orbit around the whorled core of sunlight, all straight lines flexing into a spiral shape in a universe that has no interest in rigidity and expresses itself in swelling waves, castaway conchs, and twisted strands of DNA. The sun does not attract the earth; it "bends space around itself," and the planet inevitably follows the curve.

After winning the recognition of the Royal Society, Einstein wrote an article for the London *Times* expressing his gratitude to the English scientific community for its willingness to "test a theory that had been completed and published in the country of their enemies in the midst of war."

~ ~ ~

On its journey toward justice, the arc of the moral universe loops through the painting *It Was Beautiful* by Doug Blanchard taking the form of the bent arm and pink boa framing the blissful brown face of the first queen in the kickline at Stonewall.

It flows into the scarf of the next blond queen who watches her and laughs, and into the string of beads draped over the neck of the black queen beside her looking at the raised billy club, her smiling face registering the first hint of fear, and it spills into the long waves of the brunette with an agonized look on her face who is next in line and knows what is coming.

In the shadows behind the line are the black eyes and beaten faces of those who are throwing stones, but the dancers, arm in arm, so bright and joyous in their terror, are singing. "We are the Stonewall girls/ We wear our hair in curls."

Curls. The arc of the universe curves with hips and torsos, twirls in waves and ringlets, and reiterates itself in the kicking of synchronized legs to "hypnotoize" the boys. The arc buckles in the bent arms of the cop who raises a club and it splits into the long stride of the cop next to him rushing in, a dark band of attackers charging a riotous line of rainbow colors.

Beautiful?

It wavers like an electrical current over the boy felled by cops who lies in a fetal position on the ground and shimmers and sputters like a downed power line igniting what will happen next.

~ ~ ~

In his 2008 victory speech broadcast around the world, a newly elected President Barack Obama closed his fingers, not in a fist, but as if taking hold of the air, and said that Americans had "put their hands on the arc of history and bent it toward the hope of a better day." He later had the quotation woven into the Oval Office rug, the words of King compressing the sentiments of Theodore Parker and bent in an arc running along a hem in the most powerful office in the world. A drawn bow of language. One critic wrote that Obama did not understand the quotation or history. "The problem with this kind of thinking," the critic complained, "is that it imputes an agency to history that doesn't exist."

He must not have been looking at the President's hand.

~ ~ ~

Is justice a "river of God that is full of blessing" or a bright-eyed goddess "lying prostrate on the streets?" Is it a fistful of emptiness held up to empower a crowd? Is morality hidden in the inner workings of a universe whose laws are beyond our understanding or power to change? Or, does that impute an agency to history that doesn't exist? Who knows? I had hoped that this essay would clear things up for me, but as often happens it has sent an electrical current through my confusions. Like Theodore Parker

I can see an arc, the universe is made of them, but I don't know if it is just, don't share his faith, and cannot determine where it ends.

"Why don't you guys do something?" begged Stormé DeLarverie, the word "don't" propelling others to *do*, but Lao Tzu reminds me that the wise, humbly aware of unintended consequences, practice restraint and "act without doing anything." What is the way through this paradox? Is the river of justice a gusher pushing aside boulders or a placid stream that finds its own level among stony impediments? Is the arc of justice a stem or a scythe or is it both at once like a bow drawing opposites together?

Perhaps I am asking the wrong question, or not hearing the right one properly. When Stormé DeLarverie begs "Why *don't* you guys *do*?" she may not be calling on us to do anything at all, but to *be* something. To be true to who we are, to become our better selves. Her words may have been delivered in fury, but if they are moral, we hear in them a call for justice finer than anger, not an appeal "to our easy instincts," as Barack Obama echoing Abraham Lincoln likes to say, but "to our better angels."

"Why *don't* you guys..."

So, queens at Stonewall form a kickline doing nothing but being true to themselves.

"… *do* something?"

So, queens at Stonewall throw stones becoming who they can be by resisting type and opening unrealized possibilities in themselves.

A hand closes on the invisible arc.

The archer comes round pausing without a pause.

The ploughshare uproots savage plants.

And "Not long" echoes "How long?"

"In one year," Jerry Hoose says, separating the index fingers of both hands to measure the short span of time between Stonewall and the first Gay Rights Parade, "we went from a bunch of hidden people who fought back one night in the dark to thousands of people marching in the sunlight."

Doing as becoming.

Becoming taking any shape: space bending to sun, lake yielding to mountain, glass melting in flames, a crowd shoving back against clubs.

"Yes, but they love each other," I said into the dark.

~ ~ ~

By the time Alice and Namrata announced their engagement, the arc passed through us and time, helped by a lot of talk, had worked its magic. We loved them both and fully endorsed the idea, even though marriage was a commitment that brought complications for them to sort through. It would involve living together, managing finances, handling religious differences, arranging a stunning Hindu/Unitarian wedding in the North Carolina mountains, and eventually having children. But Namrata, like Alice, was charming, smart, funny, and beautiful, and together they beamed.

"I'm just glad they're happy," you said, when we bought the sculpture at the Glass Studio, the lake behind us settling into the lap of the hills. Later at home beside the bowed window, the arc of the universe swirls at the fingertips of Alice as she passes the engagement gift to Namrata who holds it up to the light. Strings of color like the dying threads of fireworks locked in glass follow the curves, a reminder of what happens to any straight lines in our universe. Like the torso of a dancer, it twists in the glow, thrusting a muscular loop of rainbow-colored glass toward us, lit from within by the furnace of its creation.

ECLIPSING THE BRAND

The Great American Eclipse passed over my hometown, Blairsville, Georgia, on August 21, 2017, and was not only celebrated, but sold. The Chamber of Commerce sponsored three viewing parties: the Moon Party at Meeks Park, the Blairsville Industrial Park party near the airport, and the Total Tailgate party at the high school. "Credence Clearwater Revival's 'Bad Moon Rising' blared on the city's sound system," the *North Georgia News* reported, "as Eclipse Party watchers celebrated the historic event." The Eclipse Shindig at Rustic Mountain Décor kicked off a ten-day "Total Eclipse Saving Event" featuring live fiddle and guitar music from the "SeaNotes" while kids danced with tambourines and other noisemakers.

I counted twelve commercial events in our area including the Eclipse Party at Nani's Cuban Restaurant, The Solar Eclipse Block Party & Farm-to-Table Luncheon at The Sawmill Place, and The Great Eclipse Weekend at Walnut Hollow Ranch. At Trackrock Stables, guests enjoyed the Eclipse by Horseback as they trotted across the 250-acre property advertised as a "paradise of meadows, hayfields, and woodlands." At the Sit, Sip, and Watch, the Eclipse party at Hightower Creek Vineyard, customers tipped back glasses of Chatuga White, Red Clay Rosé, and Dueling Banjos Red while the Upper Hiawasee Highlands, promoted as one of the highest elevations in Georgia, darkened at mid-day under the blazing corona.

It was a chance for visitors "to see Blairsville," said the Chamber Tourism Director Tobie Chandler, and that is true, but it was more than that, much, much more. The Great American Eclipse may have been a thing of beauty, but it was also a way of peddling the brand of every city along its shadowy path. To lure visitors to "plan a trip back here later" as Chandler hopes, the businesses of Blairsville promoted the perception of my hometown as fun and rustic, a place where you can trot to a woodland clearing in the mountains, fiddle to the tap of a tambourine, or sip chardonnay while waiting romantically for the heavens to darken.

~ ~ ~

Product branding has been with us since the ancient Egyptians put irons in the fire to sear the hide of their livestock, but in our time it has become a ubiquitous feature of American life. We brand water, aromas, and dirt. We wear brands, drive brands, and sleep in brands, and, as we learned during the Great American Eclipse, we even brand the movements of celestial objects. In many ways, modern branding has not only changed the way we perceive the world around us, it has redefined what perception means. From a branding perspective, a perception is not an experience but an opinion created for us, a carefully packaged idea about an experience that is delivered to us primarily through advertising. The way I perceive the eclipse, according to those who promote it as a product, is as an abstraction that those who manage the brand shape for me.

It begins with the name: Great American Eclipse. It sounds like a campaign slogan and echoes the most consequential brand slogan of our time, "Make America Great Again," appealing to patriotism. There is, as well, the sense of a campaign within some of the other language used to promote the brand: "a total eclipse from coast to coast" the website declares, suggesting the sweep of a landslide election. "The sight of a lifetime, don't miss it!" it shouts like a carnival barker. The logo—a red, white, and blue map of the United States with a white stripe representing the path of the eclipse running across it—reinforces the message of a large country unified by greatness, and the yellow and black badge of totality that adorns the white stripe cinches the idea like a presidential seal.

As I poke around the website for the Great American Eclipse, though, I see that the message is more than a campaign slogan or a barker's pitch. The site hopes to convey the splendor and rarity of the event as well, using the stunning photograph of a "corona surrounded by iridescent clouds," for instance taken from a ship in Polynesia 1909 or a remarkable video of the "ecstasy of catching totality" filmed during the 2012 Saros expedition to Cook Shire County in Australia. American greatness, in this extension of the brand, draws on a global grandeur and accepts this rare event as a benediction from the universe. It is true that the website advertises three "eclipse themed organic wines: Totality Sparking Wine, Umbra Zinfandel, and Umbra Chardonnay" created in partnership with Frey Vineyards as well as a "Corona Glows in the Dark" t-shirt and a t-shirt with the image and logo of the Great American Eclipse emblazoned on it, but the commercialism cannot quite erase the beauty and genuine enthusiasm of the whole site. It is a marketing win-win which can place totality and tawdriness side by side without completely destroying either.

The maps on the site add more complexity to the message. There must be three dozen of them displayed in various places, including an animated "fly over" map that allows me to ride the shadow of the eclipse as it crosses the features of the American landscape. These innovative maps lend the thrill of a journey or expedition to the brand at the same time that they remind me that this is not an expedition to an unfamiliar place, but the sun and the moon conspiring to make our familiar place suddenly strange. The maps have a geological authority to them and create an imperative that is echoed in another one of the site's slogans: "where will *you* be on August 21, 2017?" No matter which state you are in, whether it is red or blue, you can participate in greatness, the maps declare appealing to bi-partisanship. But they are also, in the gradations of their lovely pastels, very beautiful. They say that the eclipse is an interplanetary event that will happen to our planet as a way of uniting a divided America, and it will be gorgeous.

In all these ways, the brand of the Great American Eclipse draws on the grandeur of the universe, and, of course, Blairsville draws on it.

~ ~ ~

What is easily overlooked in all the hoopla is the other, more ordinary, meaning of perception which is to have the experience itself unfiltered, except perhaps by darkened glasses, and, when the time is right, to remove the glasses too and watch it with the naked eye. After all, to *see* the eclipse, most of us in my home town simply had to step out of our houses at 2:35 p.m. and look up. Perceiving in this way means using my senses to apprehend the world around me as a check on the opinions and packaged perceptions that bombard me daily, and it is a daily miracle. In a way, when I left my porch, donned my solar glasses, and gazed as the moon clipped a sliver out of the sun, I was declaring my independence from the Great American Eclipse. Once the event finally began, and I turned off the computer and my cell phone, I felt free to make it my own.

Or, in part my own. That sense of liberation, the feeling that my perception belongs to me, is only part of the story because the event, even in its raw, unbranded form, is not mine to claim. The act of perceiving, as the philosopher Maurice Merleau-Ponty insisted, is charged with meaning that guides my perception. The fact that my eye is drawn to a certain object as I look about, seeing it now as the figure against the rest that is background, is a negotiation with a world that is not entirely in my control. Some objects "stand out" as the mind forms outlines of meaning around them, Merleau-Ponty argued, while others naturally recede. "The different parts of the whole—for example the portions of the figure nearest to the background—possess a particular *significance*," that reaches out to us he explained in *Phenomenology of Perception*. He called this common, human phenomenon *sens*.

But information branding the Great American Eclipse and when it would happen swamped this ephemeral idea of perception as direct interaction between me and a diminishing sun. "It's hard to believe that people used to be surprised by solar eclipses," I joked with my kids when we began making preparation for the big event. "I can't imagine anyone under this shadow who does not know it's coming." But even though I was primed for the experience, I was surprised at some level when it happened, and I did what comes naturally, I think. I let the scene guide me. When I saw the landscape turning shadowy, it made sense for my eyes to turn to the sun. Let me be precise about this moment. As the world darkened like a curtained room around me, I did not look at my watch. Instead, I followed the clues back to the source, and even though I knew what the source would be, I didn't pick out the sun. It called to me from the dusky sky, and I turned my head its way. Like a perception during a sleight of hand, my eye was guided by purposes beyond my control. I was not, literally or figuratively, the star, here. Nor was my country with the dark streak rushing across it. The sun was. In this way, simple human perception not only protects me from branding, it also protects me from myself. It is, as the scholar Lawrence Hass argues in *Merleau-Ponty's Philosophy*, "our perpetual deliverance from narcissism."

~ ~ ~

Brands became insidious in the1980s. Naomi Klein in *No Logo: Taking Aim at the Brand Bullies* calls the change "brand equity mania" and it came about when companies realized that the brand name was worth more than the products it produces. When Phillip Morris bought Kraft for six times its worth in 1988, she argues, the corporate executives and investors realized that "advertising spending was more than just a sales strategy: it was an investment in cold hard equity." To repair the cigarette company's unhealthy image with a wholesome one, the brand had to be "managed" and the entire company had to be "oriented" to serve it. Branding was no longer about pushing individual products, but instead about "extending the brand" and solidifying the company's position with its target audience. Companies scoured the planet for products to sponsor. "In the process, virtually nothing," Klein adds, had "been left unbranded." At one point, Pepsi hoped to put its logo on the face of the moon, and even though that did not happen, it only makes sense that the Great American Eclipse would be next.

I'm reminded of Bill McKibben who argued in 1989, about the time that the branding mania was getting started, that we had destroyed the concept of nature as pristine by putting the human imprint everywhere. Walking deep into the woods near where he lived, he paused by a small waterfall to wring dry his socks and realized that the creek rose and fell according to the amount of chemicals humans had injected into the atmosphere. The waterfall in essence wore our name on its shimmering hide. He called it "The End of Nature." Every creature on the planet crossed the dotted lines of human ownership, and every plant felt the effect of human activity when we turned a wild and uncultivated planet into a garden with our names dangling from a stem of each plant like a price tag. You would think that the sun, unlike our desecrated planet, would be beyond our longest branding iron, but as the Great American Eclipse shows, it is not.

Built into this process of branding, inevitably, is distortion. The idea is to put the brand between us and the product so that we purchase the brand, not the thing itself. We see that sad truth in the master of branding, the Prevaricator-in-Chief, who became the most powerful person in the world by hawking his brand instead of himself. "We have Trump steaks," the presidential candidate said standing in front of a line of American flags on the campaign trail looking like a drummer in his long, red tie. "If you want to take one we'll charge you—what?—about fifty bucks a steak," he added as a joke. It was the night of his Michigan and Mississippi primary victories, so he was in a good mood. He pointed to his wines which he claimed came from "the largest winery on the east coast." He bragged that he owned it "100%" with "no mortgage" and "no debt." Unfortunately, the steak company had gone out of business ten years before the primary night. "We've not been selling these kinds of steaks for almost 10 years now," Nehl Horton, a spokesman for the company that supplied the beef said. As for the winery, Trump does not own it, he lent his name to it, and it is not the largest on the east coast. When he speaks, he creates a perception of his brand, but it is nothing more than a euphemism for an inflated and distorted image. Over time these distortions can destroy the thing itself which goes a long way toward explaining what we have done to our country and the planet.

~ ~ ~

True perception is not an idea thrust upon us this way. It is a participatory experience: a gift offered freely and accepted graciously. When I focus my perception, I take in the sense of things the way my granddaughter, Anna, makes her way up a colorful climbing toy. "You can do it," I say, letting go of her hand. She steps up to the gaudy blue and yellow plastic contraption that extends well above both of us and seeing a blue bar sticking out just overhead realizes, without really thinking about it but by seeing, that it is for her hand. Looking down, shifting the focus by following one of the side tubes, she sees another bar about knee level and realizes that it is for her foot. As she works her way up the ladder, she discovers that what was once for her hand is now for her foot and laughs. She sees a large cylinder above her with handles in it and understands, by perceiving, that she can use the hand slots and pull her body through the cylinder. That is the fun of it. That is why she is giggling. "I can do it, Grandpa!" she announces. By *seeing*, in the sense of understanding as well as looking, she can *do*.

To look, for Merleau-Ponty, was not watching like a spectator, but an "awakening to the world," he wrote in *The Visible and the Invisible*, a dynamic process that eludes the abstractions of science. The figure of speech he settled on was perception as flesh, a figure so powerful for him it functioned like an idea. He liked the pure carnality of it. He liked the words associated with flesh because they grounded his thought, words such as corporeality, mass, and surface that occur throughout his writing. He also liked the sense of reversibility that flesh implies: when Anna grabs a handle, it in a sense is reciprocating by being grabbable, a kind of handshake from the reality outside of herself. In this way she is drawn deeper into the world.

In the end, though, the metaphor of flesh, like all metaphors, breaks down because perception is not merely physical. "Flesh is not matter, is not mind, is not substance." What it describes lies, like the space above the grasping fingers of Anna, somewhere between thing and idea. In *The Visible and the Invisible* he tried on various phrases to catch it—a "general principle," an "exemplar," or "a concrete emblem of a general manner of being"—but these all fall flat to me, never rising above the level of abstractions. When he discusses sublimation, the evaporation of a solid directly into the air, I get a sense of the ephemeral nature of the concept. But to me it is something that happens, not something that is. It is whatever is going on during the moment when Anna's hand hovers in indecision about what to do next and the delight she feels when she grabs the bar.

It happens the moment I take off the glasses, look about me at a shimmering world, and follow the impulse that the solar system I live in is sending me to look up at totality.

This is between me and that star, and it has nothing to do with the Great American Eclipse.

~   ~   ~

During the eclipse many in my family gathered at my house to see the totality. My son, Matt, and his boy, Owen, drove down from Virginia. Sam brought his two girls, Anna and Caroline, from Kennesaw. My daughter, Alice, and her partner, Namrata, came from midtown Atlanta. We had all read that even glancing at the eclipse too soon for a few seconds could do serious damage by basically cooking the image of the sun on the retina, damage that usually cannot be repaired. The day before the eclipse we gathered in the den for a trial run, and Sam asked Anna to put on her eclipse glasses and look up, and, of course, the two-year-old had them on whopper jawed with one eyeball clearly uncovered. That would never do. So Matt, Namrata, Alice, and I contrived a plan.

To view the eclipse safely we repurposed a music stand that I keep downstairs to act as a mini-observatory. We attached a set of bird-watching binoculars to the top of the stand aiming downward and taped a sheet of manila cardboard to the stand's bottom lip. The idea was to project the image of the sun onto the manila page. The afternoon before the eclipse we carried our contraption into the side yard and ran a test aiming the binoculars toward the sun, and it worked. A circular image about the size of a quarter appeared on the page. We all agreed that it would be safer for the grandchildren to view the eclipse this way. Since I had two binoculars and more stands, we went inside and made another right away.

On the day of the eclipse, we hauled our viewing equipment into the yard. Namrata and Alice set up one stand and I did the other, and as the eclipse started, I saw a small nick in the circle on the page. The event had begun. Some of us still used the glasses. Sam, Matt, Owen, and Barbara stood in the middle of the yard and donned colorful shades looking gape-mouthed like those in audience photos of 3D films, and we had fun taking pictures of each other wearing the shades, the kids staring off because with the glasses on they could not see where the camera was. In the pergola at the edge of the yard we watched small crescent moons appear on the concrete floor and spread over the fur of Gigi, our dog.

I cannot say, during all of this fun, that we were not participating in the Great American Eclipse. Certainly, it colored our excitement. All of the family, except for Sam, his girls, and me, went to the top of the hill behind our neighbor's house for a better view of totality, and, as they climbed it, I heard a giddy, almost carnival, excitement in their voices. Owen whooped, Namrata chattered like a ten-year old girl, and Alice laughed, and much of what fueled the excitement was the hype of the event, I know. Further confirmation of the lingering effects of the Great American Eclipse brand were Sam's girls, who had grown irritable due to all of the excitement which mainly confused them. From the porch Anna complained moments before totality that she had spilled chocolate milk on her dress and wanted it changed *now*. Caroline, imitating her sister's tone, reiterated the complaint. "Daddy, Anna spilled milk on her dress."

"You aren't going to miss this, son," I whispered to Sam as we stood in the yard.

"I don't want them to miss it either."

Rushing to the porch he grabbed both of the girls up in a Daddy swoop and ran with them back to the yard telling them to look down, Caroline crying and Anna fussing all the while about her dress which she pulled away from her body in disgust.

As totality approached the world turned eerie, my backyard wavering in the filmy half-dark. The porch, the house, and the trees draped around the house seemed insubstantial in the semi-dark like a veil I could pass my hand through, and the road off to the right looping up to our driveway darkened suddenly as the shadow passed over it. Anna was sniffling, pointing to the stain on her dress, but Sam held her close, and when the sun was entirely covered, he told the girls to look up and they fell suddenly silent.

During the two minutes of totality we watched the corona shimmer around the darkened moon with naked eyes. I could hear children and grandchildren on the hill laughing and shouting. Owen ran giddily through the open field with outstretched arms yelling "the world is rippling!" But where Sam, the girls, and I stood among the now useless music stands, it was silent. I was alone with the eclipse. I stood without defenses and looked into the darkening sky as the heavens formed a fiery eyeball with a black pupil that returned my gaze. I may not have been able to get the Great American Eclipse entirely out of my mind, but, when I stripped away the glasses and looked directly at the corona, what took hold of my eyes was the wild mane of the sun itself. In the presence of the sun's crown, I was delivered from narcissism. Stars appeared as planetary objects drew near, and the eclipse was alive in me, not as someone else's idea nor as anything I could conceive in my imagination, but as a blessing from the universe pulsating on the flesh of my retina.

Gatherin' Around J. P. Fraley

When J. P. Fraley takes the amphitheater stage at the Carter Caves Campground, a hush falls over the chatty audience and everyone in the semi-circular rows of benches leans forward a little in anticipation. He sits in a chair beside Barbara Kuhns who plays harmony lines for him on her fiddle, his legs spread in a slightly open stance that looks comfortable and relaxed. He runs the bow over open strings—the tuning is fine—brings the fiddle to his chin and looks out over the group assembled around him wearing on his face an impish, almost quizzical, expression that puts us all at ease. Even before he draws on the first note of "Stepdown," one of his most familiar tunes, he has created a sense of intimacy among us all. Gathered here for a Friday concert, in the presence of one of America's finest old-time fiddlers, we feel welcome and at home.

We are at the "J.P. Fraley Mountain Music Gatherin'" that has been held annually in early fall at the Carter Caves Campground in eastern Kentucky for the last thirty-two years. First organized by Annadeene Fraley, J.P.'s wife, it is a celebration of old-time music that attracts players and fans from around the country. Few of the musicians are well-known nationally—they include Bob Buckingham, Alan Freeman, Sunset Dawn, and the Reed Island Rounders among others—but for folks gathered here these are performers who keep the old songs of the mountains alive. Chief among them is Fraley himself, a small, spry man in his late seventies who has won many old-time fiddle contests at places like Fiddler's Cove, North

Carolina, and Clifftop, West Virginia, conducted workshops in fiddling all over the United States and in Ireland, and was named an "Appalachian Treasure" by Morehead State University in Kentucky.

Once J.P. begins to play, the impishness gives way, shifting to the alert and wary expression of a traveler looking far ahead for a bend in the tune. On stage he is always listening, his ears cocked. There is, in his demeanor and in the expressions that shift across his face, the look of someone searching. "I hear the note in my head before I ever touch it," he explains, and with each held note there is a patience: a love of the held sound and a reluctance to let it go, especially on the upstrokes, the hesitancy built into the way the tune unfolds in his mind. When he does, at last, take the note, his right hand bounces happily at the down stroke as if with the joy of discovery. J.P.'s style is called "expressive"—a word that conveys the patient but playful attention he brings to each phrase—and the music floats from him out into the gathering, drawing us all in, the tune taking us on an all-too-brief journey far from our earthbound days before bringing us back home again fulfilled.

The next day I'm on the road to J. P.'s house located on a hillside on a piece of his father's land. I follow directions that Barbara Kuhn has written up for me: heading south at an exit on I-64 near Grayson to a winding road. I pass small communities of clapboard houses, cross two one-lane bridges, looking for yellow buildings that mark the next turn. On my right tobacco fields stretch to the line of trees, the leaves green despite the drought, and beyond those fields the next ridge of hills that hem in this place. Eventually I find J. P.'s road which gives way to gravel as it winds deep into Hogshead Hollow. I pass a cemetery and see on my left a large embankment supported by railroad ties where the road forks into a driveway that takes me to his cabin on the hill. He and his dog, Chigger, greet me while family and musician friends stand behind him, all smiling.

The trip back to this green spot feels more like a return than a journey, a peeling back of layers, not to an older time—J. P.'s cabin is relatively new and he and his family thoroughly modern—but to a present that finds joy and love more bountiful by being grounded firmly in a place that has a past. His daughter, Michelle, is there, and Shelley who often drops by to help, and the guitarist, Robin Kessinger, whose uncle played fiddle with J.P., a protective circle. All of them love the man—I can see that in the way that they tease him and watch out for him—but they also know what he does with the fiddle and know, as well, what that thread of sound winding through all their lives means, binding them to each other and to those who came before and will come after. They know that, for now, this thread forms a lovely loop around this one old man.

J. P.'s musical education began when he heard his father whistle fiddle tunes while working, no mean feat. "Have you ever tried to whistle a fiddle tune?" J. P. says shaking his head. "I'd stick with him all day just a-listening to him working and humming and whistling." Richard Fraley was "a front porch fiddler." He sold real estate and ran various businesses, but on weekends, musicians from the surrounding area came to his house to play. "They'd come from Olive Hill and so forth. They'd all gang up and have a fiddlin' on the front porch." The young Jesse Presley Fraley—later called J.P. by almost everyone—would listen and absorb the sounds. "It meant a lot to me," he explains.

When he was nine or ten, he got a 'tater-bug' mandolin, a simple instrument with an oval shaped body tuned like a violin, and began picking out tunes for himself. The fiddle was "off-limits"—a precious item in the household that children were not supposed to touch—but J.P. was the only one of Richard Fraley's fourteen sons and daughters to show an interest in music, and eventually his father took him "under his wing" and introduced him to the mysteries of the instrument. "When I started playing tunes," J. P. explains, "I had a whole new world to play in."

His father even let him get out of chores to practice. "Dad," the young J. P. would say as the family hauled corn in the muggy summer heat, "I believe if I was down home I could play 'Sally Goodin' on the fiddle," and his father would let him go, despite his resentful brothers. "I had my mind more on skinny dipping than anything," J. P. admits. He would get his dad's fiddle from its place under the bed, remove the cloth case, and play for about five minutes until he got "Sally Goodin'" down and then head off for the river at the lower end of the farm to swim with his friends, getting back in time for his hair to dry before his dad and brothers got home. "They'd think I had been playing all day."

J. P.'s father took him to hear the best fiddlers in the area including Ed Haley, the blind street musician from Ashland, Kentucky, that J. P. calls the "Sage of Fiddling." Haley's granddaughters would lead him to street corners in Ashland where the fiddler played for tips. After giving Haley some money, J. P.'s father would instruct the musician to play while his son listened, insisting only that he play "Billy in the Lowground" along the way. J. P. would stay for hours. Passersby and shopkeepers often abused Haley, and J. P. remembers some merchants kicking the musician's feet to get him to move on. "I got so mad," J. P. says angrily. "He was just a genius."

Haley played the fiddle in the old-fashioned way, holding it on his chest rather than under his chin. He would often rock the violin back and forth beneath the bow as he played, a technique that allowed him to create nuanced and subtle tones from the fiddle. "He could make a dark fiddle talk with his short strokes up with the bow," J. P. explains.

"Nobody else I know could do it—as if the tune had words."

For J. P., Haley's sound was the epitome of expressive playing. "I've heard the most prominent fiddlers as we know them today," J. P. explained in a brief autobiographical sketch that accompanied his first recording, but "I don't think any of them could equal Ed Haley."

J.P. met his best friend and musical collaborator when, at age sixteen, he fell in love with Annadeene Prater from Star Branch. She was only fourteen when he saw her in the schoolyard getting off of a bus. Pictures from the time show a dark-eyed girl with a fondness for bows and flowers in her dark hair. I show J. P. one photograph of her holding a guitar and standing beside a friend and sense the emotions gathering in him. She is wearing a jumper and a white blouse and looks into the camera with a half-smile, a knobby knee showing just under her skirt hem. J. P. studies the picture, saying nothing at first. "When Annadeene got off the bus, she wasn't nothing but heel strings and eyeballs," he says finally, "just a leggy kid, but I thought she was the prettiest thing I'd ever seen." He hands the picture back to me. "It never did change."

Annadeene was an accomplished musician, "one of the Rachel Valley Girls that played over at WCMI in Ashland all the way through high school." She loved singing close harmonies and was particularly good on the guitar. "Annadeene was musically intelligent," J. P. says. "She knew how to get the sound out of the guitar to match the fiddle." Eventually she and J. P. eloped in Maysville and settled down to raise a family, and, for a while music was put on hold. "We got busy raising a family. We had four children, three girls and a boy." It wasn't until the children had gotten older that J. P. borrowed a guitar for Annadeene, and the two of them entered a contest that would give their lives a new direction.

"Tell me about the contest where the fiddle exploded," I ask.

"We had gone to the contest more or less as a joke," J. P. said. It was held in the little town of Flatwoods, Kentucky—where "both city limit signs hang on the same post"—but it drew fiddlers from as far away as Nashville. He had borrowed a guitar for Annadeene from a local dealer promising that if he won, he would buy it for her. His own fiddle was held together with a clothespin on the tailpiece. The contest came down to a playoff between a flashy Nashville fiddler and J. P., and after an exchange of songs J. P. won. Less than an hour after it was over J. P. raked his bow over the strings, the clothespin popped off, and the bridge flew in the air. "The fiddle blowed up on me!" he said, but he didn't care. "Someone up above must have been with me."

The contest was the beginning of J. P.'s return to music—and the best part was that Annadeene returned with him. For years they played together in other contests and at concerts throughout the region and made two beautiful recordings: *Wild Rose of the Mountain* and *Maysville*. In the sixties, Annadeene decided to locate the Fraley family reunion at the Carter Caves Resort in Kentucky, and the "J. P. Fraley Mountain Music Gatherin'" was born. After Annadeene died in 1996, *Wild Rose of the Mountains* was reissued in her honor as a CD, with J. P.'s daughter, Danielle, accompanying him on new selections. Informally, the "Gatherin'" is held in Annadeene's honor as a legacy to the musical tradition she fostered. She was, as J. P. puts it, "a jewel of a woman."

I ask J. P. to play a tune. He retreats into the house to get his fiddle and returns a few minutes later with fiddle in hand and Robin Kessinger, the guitarist, in tow. J. P. picks at the strings with his finger to check the tuning. His fiddle is lovely. Made by the fiddler Jim McKillop and given to J. P. during his tour through Ireland, it has a sweet sound with a nice lower register perfectly suited to J. P.'s playing. Robin and J. P. play "Margaret's

Waltz," a tune written by the Scottish fiddler Ally Bain, a fan who often returns the favor by performing J. P.'s tunes in Ireland. As J. P. plays, he remains still, but fully animated, his face aglow and his facial expressions matching the lilt and movement of the slow waltz. The word 'effortless' first comes to mind—"If it were hard work," J. P. told me earlier, "I wouldn't do it!"—but effortlessness does not describe these motions. They are intuitive and solid and steady. He does not strike the strings or cut into them so much as lay the weight of his hand on the frog and pull the sound from the instrument. "I love waltz's," J. P. explained. "When you start your low notes it's kind of rough, but seems like it climbs into the key you want." J. P. lays into the base strings—his head slightly tilted—his bow starting at the low end of the note with a rasp and coming to pitch early, the note retrieved, it seems, from some dark well and offered up to sunshine like pure water.

When he was a boy, his father warned him of the importance of taking care of the bow while playing. "Don't lean on it too hard," he said. "It'd quarrel with you." He cautioned his son on the need to play with the whole bow, saying he could make six fiddle bows out of the young J. P.'s choppy strokes. J. P. still believes that using the whole bow leads to smooth fiddling, but he rarely swings his arms for wide and dramatic strokes. He uses the whole bow, yes, but gets to the other end eventually, never hurrying his stroke to pump up the performance or charge it with bravado. "One of the greatest things about playing with J. P." Robin tells me later, "is that he listens to everybody playing." That is the clue.

For J. P., playing music is an intense form of listening—that is what his face, with its shifting expressions, registers. It is part of his generous spirit to do so. He also remains attentive to the music in the air. "I learned the fiddle tunes in my head," he tells me, "long before I ever thought about playing them." For J. P. the instrument is not played; rather the sound is discovered in some hidden place and teased out. He is not paying attention to the fiddle, or the bow for that matter, but is alert to something far off, some resonance far away that he is coaxing into audibility.

Later that night, after the interview, I'm headed back to the Carter Caves for the Saturday evening concert. This is Kentucky limestone country and the cut hillsides on the winding road down to the park are lined with flat rocks that emerge out of the bank, trees and bushes clinging to a thin layer of soil. I never get a chance to ask J. P. directly what he thinks about the future of the music he plays. I don't think I have to. This festival is a testament to his hope for the future. He watches every act that performs on the stage while I am there and smiles as broadly for the young players, like Jake Crack, as he does for his old friends, Bo D and Jennings Morgan. "This man is a great guitarist," he says of Robin Kessinger, clearly proud of his old friend's nephew. The music grows naturally in a place like this, clinging like spindly trees to the rocky edges of modern culture. When I see Sherry Stanford's little girl dancing in front of the hotel while her mother's group, Sunset Dawn, leads a jam, I know that the call of this music is irresistible—and in good hands.

Later I make my way down to the amphitheater and find J. P. talking to his daughter, Michelle. On stage, a musician has called him a living legend—a phrase often invoked at this gathering for J. P.—and the adulation clearly makes him a little nervous, but he has decided that when his bit on stage is done, he will stay to watch the rest of the show, declining an early ride home. "I guess if you're a living legend," Michelle says with a wry smile, "you can do what you want!"

Eventually it is his time on stage again, and he and Barbara settled in for a couple of tunes. Once again, the crowd seems to lean forward, drawn to him, and when he starts to play, the night sky over Carter Caves fills with sweet melody, J. P. getting more sound per inch out of his bow than six other fiddlers could. The music sweeps over the crowd hemmed into this arena and holds us together as one. We lose ourselves to find each other, and, paradoxically, run, into our best selves along the way. We feel, among the strangers who have taken us in, welcome and at home.

THE POLITICAL PERSONAL ESSAY

Writers of the political personal essay face a challenge when they tackle a social wrong. Should they bear witness to the truth by presenting a nuanced view of experience that is suspicious of political abstractions? Or can they play an active role in shaping those abstractions and take a stand? Personal essays may be a subtle form of witnessing that resists certainty of any kind, especially political certainty—"What do I know?" Montaigne famously proclaimed, writing essays after he retired from politics—and yet some of our finest writers have taken on the challenge of an explicitly political personal essay, one that goes beyond a literature of witness to a literature of commitment modeling an appropriate response to society's ills that becomes a call for action. In fact, in American culture the personal essay has tackled our ugliest political wrongs, including slavery, racism, war, sexism, homophobia, and environmental degradation. So, how does a writer take a stand on political issues such as these while remaining true to the tentative nature and inquisitive spirit of the personal essay? The answer, I say, is to make the abstractions personal by going back to the moment of their discovery.

Let's start with a passage from one of our classic political texts, "Civil Disobedience," conceived by Henry David Thoreau during a night of solitary confinement in jail in 1846. It has probably done more to change the world for the better than any other personal essay. Believing that money for The Mexican War was an indirect way to support slavery, Thoreau refused to pay taxes, so he was carted off to jail becoming a model for many who have defied the powers that be. After a long introduction, in which he doesn't mention his own experience, he pauses to examine his jail cell and makes a discovery that shook the world.

> I stood considering the walls of solid stone, two or three feet thick, the door of wood and iron, a foot thick, and the iron grating which strained the light…. I saw that, if there was a wall of stone between me and my townsmen, there was a still more difficult one to climb or break through before they could get to be as free as I was. I did not for a moment feel confined, and the walls seemed a great waste of stone and mortar. I felt as if I alone of all my townsmen had paid my tax…. I could not but smile to see how industriously they locked the door on my meditations, which followed them out again without let or hindrance, and *they* were really all that was dangerous.

Until we reach this paragraph a little more than halfway through the text, "Civil Disobedience" is not a personal essay, but a rant full of memorable phrases. "That government is best which governs not at all," he exclaims, and "government never of itself furthered any enterprise, but by the alacrity with which it got out of its way," and "I cannot for an instant recognize that political organization as *my* government which is the *slave's* government also." And on and on. Of course, we enjoy the wit that sweeps in with this torrent, but in the paragraph about his night alone in jail Thoreau stops to take a breath and look at his surroundings—"the walls of solid stone, two or three feet thick, the door of wood and iron, a foot thick, and the iron grating which strained the light"—and the essay takes an introspective turn.

He no longer shouts at the world as he does rhetorically in the earlier part of the essay, but whispers to himself while discovering his essential truth. "I could not help but smile" he writes as a new understanding slowly dawns on him. The walls he is staring at liberate him—and pay his taxes to boot. Cut off from the people in his town by the prison gate he realizes that he is the only one free because he is following his conscience while they are enslaved to the injustice they support with their money. They may have locked the door on his "flesh and blood and bones," but his solitary meditations are the real threat, and they follow his captors out of the jail "without let or hindrance" to haunt them and others who abet social wrongs this way. What his jailers could not touch was his solitary mind, the source of all personal essays.

To me this moment of inwardness in the presence of a social wrong is the essential move in a personal political essay, its moment of truth, and no matter where it is placed it is where the essay began. Without this move, rendered for us as a small scene, the essay, no matter how personal in its events, is a public performance and not personal at all where it matters: in its discoveries as they happen. For the reader, the intimacy of watching and participating in the thought process is a privilege, and once we live through the conditions under which the thinking happened, generously reproduced by the essayist, we are more apt to see the idea anew and modify our own position and even change our minds or, if we agreed with the ideas from the start, feel less lonely in our convictions. This is the great gift that the personal essay offers our mean-spirited politics: the power of intimacy.

~ ~ ~

What I am calling for in the political personal essay is that it remain honest in the most essential way, honest to the person who writes it as she or he enters the public arena. We expect essayists to be honest about events, especially in an essay on a political issue, but more than that we ask that they are honest with themselves, revealing who they are, not just in what they do, but by letting us in on the shifts of their wayward minds as events unfold, admitting confusions and false starts on the path toward an idea.

So where did the thought process that led to this essay begin? I know that I was reluctant to write directly about political subjects early in my career—and most of the essays in the second half of this collection are earlier and shy away from overtly political subjects. But during the month of February 2017 my thinking began to evolve. I lead a panel discussion at a week-long writers' conference in Washington D.C. called "Following the Thread of Thought" about the art of reflection in personal essays, calling for a Keatsian "negative capability" which explores ideas without reaching for a position, and quoting writers like Vivian Gornick who believed that the writer's job is to mystify ideas, not clarify them. But something was stirring within me because at a reading later that night I chose a passage from an essay on how artists and ordinary, decent people should respond to political evil that would become the essay "The Beloved Republic." The conference was a heady week of panels and readings, but on one afternoon my wife and I took a break to tour the National Museum of African American History and Culture. I saw beauty in artifacts from the March on Washington on display there and solidarity made vivid in enormous panels of art from Resurrection City when activists temporarily took over the National Mall to protest hunger. "The great forge of history comes from the fact that we carry it within us, are unconsciously controlled by it," I read on a plaque quoting James Baldwin. "History is literally present in all that we do." Yes, in "all that we do." I saw the appalling display of shackles including those forged for the hands of children, thought of my own grandchildren, and was ashamed. Yes, something was stirring in me.

On the last day of the conference, Barbara and I, yearning to find a way to respond in my writing to a democracy drifting toward authoritarianism, made our way to a peaceful rally of writers at the conference. I remember the late-night glow of The White House above fencing and cement barricades and Barbara's face lit by vigil candles that organizers passed out. The speeches were disappointing—the hastily organized group of brilliant wordsmiths resorting to clichés like "power to the people," "resist," and "diversity is strength." What was missing in their oratory was their skill with written language, and it was then that I knew that I had to find a way to address public subjects in prose that clearly took a stand but remained subtle and, above all, personal. In a notebook I wrote that "it is the chameleon process of art that makes it subversive of conventional thinking and a state run on platitudes." When I got home, I reread personal essayists with a political bent who had moved me in the past and began this essay.

~   ~   ~

I started with James Baldwin who had opened my eyes about racism when I was young. In "Notes of a Native Son," he reveals his mental, political, and spiritual anguish about the death of his father and the birth of his sister on the same day amid race riots when he was nineteen. He describes his father as a cruel man given to bigotry and largely destroyed by the burden of his racial animus and remembers in the essay that same hatred welling up in himself and culminating in an awful night when he threw a mug at a white waitress who told him "We don't serve Negroes here," flirting with a disaster he barely escaped. Now his father is dead. He has gazed into the casket at the funeral and seen the powdered face of an old man who could no longer hurt anyone. As he sits in the car on the way to the gravesite, anger smoldering within him, he ponders a passage from the *Book of Joshua* in the Bible about choosing between the God of the oppressors and the God of the fathers.

> I suspected in these familiar lines a meaning which had never been there for me before. All of my father's texts and songs, which I had decided were meaningless, were arranged before me at his death like empty bottles, waiting to hold the meaning which life would give them for me. This was his legacy: nothing is ever escaped. That bleakly memorable morning I hated the unbelievable streets and the Negroes and whites who had, equally, made them that way. But I knew that it was folly, as my father would have said, this bitterness was folly.

The writer at the crux of the essay withdraws from the world to brood over events on the way to making a crucial discovery. The Biblical passage that he and his father had used in sermons, glows golden in his memory and takes on new meaning now that his father is gone. It insists that he choose between a God of righteous fury or calm acceptance. This choice, and its consequences waiting like empty vessels to be filled, is the paternal legacy that he cannot escape and, as he contemplates it, he is transformed, changing his mind before our reading eyes, realizing that his hatred is a dangerous folly, and in that discovery he begins to sort out what he could stake his life on and what he must reject: "It was necessary to hold on to the things that mattered. The dead man mattered, the new life mattered; blackness and whiteness did not matter; to believe that they did was to acquiesce in one's own destruction. Hatred, which could destroy so much, never failed to destroy the man who hated and this was an immutable law."

We know the scene unfolding before the young Baldwin as he makes these discoveries because it was described on the opening page of the essay. The family drove to the graveyard "through a wilderness of smashed plate glass" from the Harlem riots. While looking at the desolation and pondering the new life of his sister and the death of his father, the moment of lyrical introspection in the car leads to a stunning paradox that concludes the essay, the necessary but impossible proposition that he must choose to follow *both* gods and live according to contrary principles: accepting life with its myriad evils "totally without rancor" while never becoming complacent in the face of those evils by resisting them "with all one's strength."

The choice is to accept *and* resist. Without acceptance there is no hope for love, and without resistance there is no hope for justice, an intriguing insight, but notice that the paradox when explained baldly that way is empty, even banal. What we need is the *agon*, Baldwin's struggle as he reckons with the death of his father and his own guilty past as well as the birth of his sister and the hope for love in the future. What we need is the essay, artfully constructed, which allows us to watch the idea in all its complexity unfold in the writer as he responds to events. It is not pure mind at work—this is not analytic philosophy—but the mind in context, in flux amid apparently irreconcilable conflicts where the self is forged. It is that self in the process of forming that we as readers insist the personal essayist be true to when writing on a political evil like racism.

~ ~ ~

In the late 1980's Bill McKibben declared "The End of Nature" in an essay by that name supplying convincing evidence for his case from experts and writers in the popular press, but in the end, the essay is personal as well as political, and the moment of insight—his realization that what we once thought of as nature no longer exists—happened during a day-long hike that he took by himself along Mill Creek that runs near his property in the Adirondacks. It was not wilderness—along the way he came upon some creekside kitchen chairs that his neighbors set out for fishing and later bought a liverwurst sandwich at a store—but most of it was rough going. The stream meandered and he had come without a machete to clear away the nameless briars that blocked his path. Here and there as he walked, he emerged from the woods scratched and sore and often thought of turning back, but pressed on finding gifts along the way: "a vein of quartz," "a ridge where the maples still held their leaves," and a pine that beavers had gnawed into "a forty-foot sculpture."

He stopped at a waterfall remembering when Mill Creek had flooded several years earlier and his awe standing there realizing "what nature is capable of" as the ground below him trembled. But now the falls, tamed by drought, flowed quietly, one of those "diaphanous-veil affairs" he calls it, and as he stopped to change his socks from a "soaking" pair to one "merely clammy," he saw "nothing awe inspiring or instructive, or even lulling, in the fall of the water." He realized that what he was watching looked "less like a waterfall than like a spillway to accommodate the overflow of a reservoir." It was still beautiful, but what it meant to him had shifted from the days when he experienced it as a torrent. He knew that the rain and snow that produced the water was influenced by "the particular mix of chemicals we've injected into the atmosphere" and felt suddenly lonelier.

What McKibben is about to discover is that the idea of nature as a wonder separate from us has come to an end, an insight that has grave social implications.

> Instead of a world where rain had an independent and mysterious existence, the rain had become a subset of human activity: a phenomenon like smog or commerce or the noise from the skidder towing logs on Cleveland Road—all things over which I had no control, either. The rain bore a brand; it was a *steer*, not a *deer*. And that was where the loneliness came from. There's nothing there except us. There's no such thing as nature anymore—that other world that isn't business and art and breakfast is now not another world, and there is nothing except us alone.

He realizes that the rain which produces the waterfall at his wet feet is a "subset of human activity" influenced by all that humans emit into the atmosphere, and the voice of nature from a world elsewhere that had chastened and once guided writers like Thoreau is lost in the human chatter. The waterfall may be beautiful and remote, and we do not control it, but its meaning has changed because it no longer has some "mysterious" existence apart from humankind.

As he mulls over his discovery, the images of the stream and waterfall give way to synecdoches for the insinuation of human activity into the natural world, the smog-corrupted air standing in for the effects of commerce in general and "the noise from the skidder towing logs on Cleveland Road" evoking the clatter of all human activity around the world. Unlike the "deer" that lives in the wild, nature has become a "steer" altered and corralled for human purposes. Often used by writers to universalize their experience, the synecdoche that lets a part stand for the whole is a fitting device for moving from a personal epiphany to its larger social implications. So, in that list of what nature has become—"business and art and breakfast"—the word "breakfast," which transforms nourishment into a human social event, carries the load for everything that we have domesticated.

His emotional response to this discovery, an indulgence which the personal essay affords, is mixed. First, he feels a particular kind of loneliness, "one that corresponds to the cry 'What will I do without him?' when someone vital dies." In this sense his journey to a place where he is alone, contemplating a veil of water, is an appropriate setting for his grief at the loss of nature as a source of wonder. At the same time, despite being alone in the woods, he feels "crowded, without privacy" because in a world where there is nothing *except* us there is no escape *from* us. When he looks at the sick trees in the woods around him on his walk, he cannot escape the excuses spoken by businessmen and politicians who profit from the damage or the voices of his friends and neighbors who enjoy cars, air-conditioning, and shopping. Above all he cannot escape himself. "I live on about four hundred times what Thoreau conclusively proved was enough," he confesses, "so I've done my share to take this independent, eternal world and turn it into a science project." As fury and indignation in the face of evil well up in him, a corresponding sense of melancholy about his own complicity and the human condition in general tempers the anger without diluting the call to action. Later, when he expands the essay into a book, he offers ways to defy and resist consumerism and ameliorate the damage. Contemplating the consequences of what we have done, he reconsiders the phrase "greenhouse effect" used to describe heat trapped by rising levels of carbon dioxide in the atmosphere. "We have built a greenhouse," he laments, weighing the implications, "where once there bloomed a sweet and wild garden."

~ ~ ~

In "The Clan of One-Breasted Women" Terry Tempest Williams and nine other conspirators "slipped under a barbed-wire fence" to sneak into Mercury, Nevada, a closed town so contaminated by atomic waste from the nearby Nevada Test Site that pregnant women and children were not allowed to enter. Williams and her accomplices were trespassing, protesting atomic testing conducted in northern Utah by the United States government since the 1950's. The tests had led to increased cancer rates in a region largely inhabited by Mormons and Native Americans. The protestors moved deliberately through a grove of Joshua trees at the outskirts of town and waited. At dawn they wrapped themselves in mylar with their faces exposed and moved through Mercury like winged creatures. Invoking Thoreau, Williams calls this incursion an "act of civil disobedience" on behalf of cancer victims, the "Clan of One-Breasted Women." She and the others were arrested, and when she was handcuffed and frisked, the officer found "a pen and a pad of paper" inside her boot.

"And these?" the arresting officer asked.

"Weapons," Williams replied.

Williams sets up this scene by supplying evidence for the damage inflicted on her, her family, and her region by the atomic tests. She describes a memory of watching an atomic blast light up the desert sky from the family car when she was a child, offers testimony by plaintiffs in a damage case, provides information about downwind fallout and increased cancer rates, and movingly writes about the death of her mother and other women in her family to breast cancer as well as her own cancer. In short, she explains herself, makes her case, and dramatizes it by telling the story of the protest, culminating in her arrest and ending with her glib remark about the officer finding her weapons: her pen and pad.

On the bus-ride out of town after her arrest, though, she drops the sarcasm and grows contemplative. Looking out of the bus window at the familiar landscape, she recalls a time in the desert with her mother, and her voice turns lyrical.

> The Joshua trees standing their ground had been named by my ancestors, who believed they looked like prophets pointing west to the Promised Land. These were the same trees that bloomed each spring, flowers appearing like white flames in the Mojave. And I recalled a full moon in May, when Mother and I had walked among them, flushing out mourning doves and owls.

Here, the experience ends and the essay, written presumably with her pen on that pad, begins. These trees that bloom in the desert claim the land by "standing their ground" and point hopefully toward a better world. At the same time, they give her a personal glimpse of a lost past when she and her mother "walked among them" encompassing the political in a memory and going beyond it.

As the conflict goes internal, the writer realizes what is at stake and reaches deep for eloquence. Desert "flowers" are compared to white "flames," the words alliterating. "Mojave" and "May" and "Mother" alliterate too, calling attention to themselves with capital letters as well as "moon" and "mourning" tucked in in lower case. There is a hush in the phrase "flushing out" and the word "bloom" coos like a dove or owl. It is here, in a brief passage of lyric prose, that the loss, defiance, and hope for a better world at the heart of her essay are intensified and embodied, suggesting the substance of these themes without burdening them with explanation. It is her weapon, yes, the pen and pad another synecdoche, but it is not primarily a weapon for convincing others of her ideas. It is a tool for mining the self where commitment is forged.

~ ~ ~

I still don't know exactly where to draw the line between witnessing and commitment in personal essays. I go case by case, feeling my way along a seam of language toward the solitary moment of a discovery. But the writers I turned to after my trip to Washington D.C. reminded me that art leads the way. I think of the ambiguous beauty of "the iron grating which strained the light" fortifying Thoreau, the barred window redefined as a vehicle for the free expression of controversial ideas, or the "wilderness of smashed plate glass" in Baldwin, a metonymy for the riots that by the end of his essay comes to stand for breakthrough as well as breakdown. I think of the word "greenhouse" unforgettably transformed by McKibben from a brittle palace of glass to a chamber emptied of wonder that has fueled a lifetime of activism.

Art leads the way for me as a reader, too, the silence after I close the book insisting that I act even as it reminds me that the true struggle is not about winning or losing in an imperfect world. It is about following the dictates of a newly pricked conscience and having the grace to accept the consequences. The opposite of propaganda, it sets me precariously on an edge where personal witnessing and political commitment face off, and holds me there enchanted and provoked. Supported by narrative, exposition, and commentary these interior reckonings are a way, perhaps the most authentic way, for individuals to confront society and change minds. I know that I could not have written about race in "The Other Steve Harvey" without reading Baldwin and understanding the nearly impossible position of both acceptance and resistance that whites like me, blind to hidden bias, put African Americans like him in. Without reading about McKibben's epiphany at the waterfall, I would not have understood that putting the human brand on the natural world is the end of nature and could not have written about it in "Eclipsing the Brand." Reading Thoreau's "Civil Disobedience" while I was a freshman in college, a time of youthful protests for equality and peace, set the stage for "Madre Luz" and its conclusion about icons of peaceful protest in the past.

In all cases, art animates ideas, making palpable the issues that led to essays in this book: unconscious bias, gun violence, creeping authoritarianism, an economic system that threatens life on the planet, and, above all, the fate of justice in a world that seems hell-bent on evil. I will still write personal essays full of questions and ambiguities, I'm sure, but I will no longer shy away from those that require an unequivocal political stance. It may seem surprising that a political personal essay would turn lyrical, even poetic, given the urgency of its message, a kind of indulgence in a grubby and corrupt world, but that is precisely what we need during troubled times, an aria getting us through the night and pointing in the morning to the Promised Land.

A Laying on of Hands

A dark slick rising and falling in silky waves caught my eye. Some dusky residue of night. The sun had just risen above the Florida Gulf, igniting the sky momentarily in pinks and reds and giving definition to the dunes and sea oats all about me while the house, the wooden walkway, even my arms turned golden in the glow. The water, that lay placid and still against the bowed horizon, culminated along the beach in a hush of long, perfect waves. I had been sitting in a beach chair strumming a ukulele when the black shape appeared—materialized, it seemed, in folds of blue— undulating with the water. I set my instrument down and stood to get a better look, shading my eyes. Suddenly a shape like a wind-lifted lapel emerged briefly out of the spray, and I knew that the darkness I saw could not be a shadow, but an object of some kind, though the movement seemed involuntary, more the rocking of the lovely and indifferent semi-tropical waters than a thing alive.

I did not realize at first that the shape rolling in the water was a whale, a baby sperm whale to be exact, but I did walk down to the water's edge and on closer look saw that it was a large sea creature. Most of the enormous body lay hidden under water that was slowly turning azure in the morning sun, but I saw the tail clearly, the black lapel, that roiled with the waters and, when a breaker tumbled in, rose out of the wave with a gush and slapped back at the sea. We had often seen dolphins play here, St. George Island is famous for them, so I thought it might be a dolphin though it looked far too large. Recently we had heard reports of sharks attacking children at the water's edge so that thought glided ominously through my mind. I kept my distance. I'm pretty sure that I was the first on the scene since I had watched the shape emerge out of the night with no one else around. After a long look, in which the body rose and fell with the swelling of the waves, I went back to my ukulele and sat in the sand, wondering what is done when an enormous, dead sea creature washes up on the beach.

~ ~ ~

But it was not dead. I walked back to the beach house. Louisa Franklin, whose family shared the St. George house with ours, was pouring coffee and blinking her eyes to wake up. Louisa is usually game for anything, even the sight of a whale at the crack of dawn, so soon she and I were headed down the beach, holding coffee mugs in front of us as we tried to negotiate the tricky sand, making our way to the spot where the whale had washed up. It still looked lifeless and out of place, like a sofa rolling on the waves, but two plucky volunteers who were in the water, their shorts wet at the hem, assured us that it was alive, breathing through its blow hole.

A small crowd had gathered by now and no one knew what to do. A day earlier this same whale had washed up further down the beach and locals had guided it back into deeper water. Some suggested that we should try to do that. Others thought that the whale was too weak to survive at sea, that it had come here to die and we should let it. Someone said that we should call the aquatic center in Clearwater. Louisa and I were about ready to head back to our house, put off by all the squabbling, when one of the women in the water shouted. "We need some help here," and we saw that she and her friend were trying to turn the whale and lift its head out of the water. "I think it's drowning!"

Not long after that I found myself in the water with twenty or thirty other people. They had turned the whale so that it faced in to shore and were holding it in their arms to keep its blow hole out of the water. Others had taken positions along the whale's body and passing blankets, towels and t-shirts underneath created a makeshift sling in order to keep the whale up out of the surf. I found a spot about half-way down the whale's body and the dark-haired man across from me passed the tail of a shirt underwater. Grabbing my end, I leaned back, hoisting the whale up a bit. I secured the t-shirt wrapping it tightly in my fingers, my knuckles turning white, and with my free hand spread water as the others were doing over the exposed hide of the whale.

How many people ever get to touch a whale! The breathing animal lay docile in the midst of all of us holding it in our hands and arms. The hide felt cold and stiff and hard like a car tire but beneath it beat the heart of a mammal which, if it lived, would grow to be one of the most magnificent creatures on earth. I twisted the t-shirt tighter in my fingers, pulled hard, and, amid the newly formed team of volunteers, waited.

~ ~ ~

Much of the majesty of sperm whales comes from their sheer size. The largest of the toothed whales, they can live seventy years, grow to be sixty feet long, and weigh fifty tons. The heart alone usually weighs two-hundred and seventy-five pounds, about the same weight as two human beings. "You definitely feel puny," one diver wrote after swimming with a whale, "when thirty tons of flesh swims by." The whale that had beached with us was a baby, only eleven feet long, but already it was larger than any animal I had ever touched. It took about twenty of us, in shifts, just to hold the body up in the water, the simple bulk of the creature making it seem alien and strange to us.

And yet it was not. After all, when the woman in the water called for help for the drowning whale most of us rushed in, and when we lifted it in a sling made from our shirts and towels and rubbed water over its hump most of us felt a mammalian kinship. The mother sperm whale nurses young calves like the one we were helping. While males roam wide across the seas of the planet, females and the young stay behind to form a kind of nursery. Mothers are loyal to their young but often depend on the group to protect them while they gather food. They sing to the calves, a form of echo-location, in order to keep track of them. The males dance in the water for the females when they return during mating season as part of the courtship ritual, in a kind of large-scale aquatic barn dance, and chant songs about their adventures far away. All of that sounds pretty familiar to me.

But the bond that I felt most was the reason that we had to help: whales breathe air. They breathe through a blow hole located near the top of their heads and can go under water for several hours at a time diving deep in a single breath in pursuit of their favorite food, the bottom-dwelling giant squid. When they emerge, they blow in a burst that can often be heard nearly a mile away. Once I was stationed right by the blow hole, a small s-shaped lip of flesh that opened and closed every three or four minutes, and I felt the warm, musty breath on my face. "Watch out for whale snot," some kid said as a joke, but the joke died among us. "Baby's breath"—that is what I thought, remembering the sweet stale odor of my own children's breath when they were nursing. Baby sperm whales drink milk, warm blood floods the chambers of their hearts, and they breathe the air. They may grow to weigh as much as a tractor trailer rig, but they are one of us.

~ ~ ~

We dubbed the whale George Barry: George for St. George Island where he had washed up and Barry for the hurricane that had drenched the area with rain the day before and had forced us all to evacuate the island. Eventually a large crowd gathered with many vacationers in swimsuits and large hats taking a turn holding the makeshift sling of blankets, towels, and t-shirts. All in my family helped and so did our friends. Many vacationers who took a turn beside the whale came from far off, Canada and the northeast as well as the south, and Louisa and her husband David who teach with me met some former students, too. An *ad hoc* community was beginning to form. Those who did not actually hold the whale brought sunscreen and water and later pizza for the group that had gathered. It was nearly dusk before experts from the Clearwater marina could arrive with a crane, so we had to stay with the task all day.

The hardest part for me was keeping my footing. Occasionally George grew restless and shifted in the water. Sometimes big breakers would crash in on us causing George, and all of his helpers, to slide to one side. Children who helped sometimes caught a face full of water when that happened, and all of us had to reposition our feet and tug on the towels and t-shirts that suspended George to keep from tipping over. My hands got stiff from holding the t-shirts tightly, and when other helpers were relieved of their posts, I noticed that they would shake their hands as they walked to the beach trying to get some life back into them.

The work never seemed hard, but soon the curiosity wore off and the drudgery of holding a position set in. Still, I noticed as the day wore on that the crowd grew bigger, not just the crowd of on-lookers, but the group of helpers as well. My friends and family and I could go back to our beach house for lunch and return a few hours later and the group with their hands on the whale never diminished. When I took a spot, I joined a team bound by nothing other than a desire to help. I remember the faces: the man with dark hair and authoritative eyes, the red-haired teenage girl with beads of water on her cheek and a dab of white sun-block on her nose, the little boy who kept getting waves in his face. Often, we had to lean back, fighting the natural drift toward the beach, and at one point the woman ahead of me was nearly in my lap, her leg against my thigh, in order to keep her towel end up high enough. We didn't talk much, just a few barked commands about our positions, but we did look into each other's eyes to keep our actions in sync, more by intuition than plan, and moved together as the waves rolled in.

Most of all, I remember the many hands gripping the sling and gently rubbing the whale. Our task was to keep the whale body low enough in the water that it would not be burned or dried out by the sun and yet high enough so that the blow hole was free to breathe. Any exposed hide had to be covered by wet towels, and our hands were used to keep the skin moist and towels in place, but there was more to rubbing the whale's back than mere utilitarian need. When I touch the hide of a whale, it touches back and, in that gesture, lies the beginnings of mutual responsibility. Our hands kept the whale alive for a while, yes, but they also received as much comfort as they gave. We were caressing the animal, our eyes opening wide with affection and awe as we rubbed, drawing on a power larger than each of us. It was a laying on of hands.

~ ~ ~

Many of the churches where I live believe in the power of the laying on of hands. I once visited one, a church that a friend of mine attends, a small chapel beyond the little town of Hiawassee, Georgia. After a Sunday school class with a video on the end of the world when the souls of the faithful would be "raptured" into heaven while the rest of us poor suckers got blown away by Armageddon, we attended the service itself. At first it seemed much like Sunday morning at the Methodist church with several announcements by the pastor and the youth leader and a few prayers, but when we got to the songs, all heaven broke loose.

Most of the members of the congregation put one or two arms in the air and began to sway. Occasionally a voice would float above the other singers in a kind of shout, an incomprehensible phrase that exploded across the room. A few of the women in different parts of the church fell where they stood, one in the center aisle, and began shivering and shaking uncontrollably in their Sunday dresses. Most of us kept on singing, though I must say that I had trouble following the tune amid all of the pandemonium, but I did watch a few members of the congregation gather around the nearest writhing woman and put a hand on her, still holding the free hand in the air, and praying aloud as the song continued. The gesture was meant as comfort, yes, but also as a drawing on the power of her spirit as well, perhaps to free it or purge it as a kind of contagious enthusiasm passed from one soul to another.

The Bible, especially parts about the ministry of Jesus and the early church, offers examples of the power of touch to transform. In Mark, a leper beseeches Jesus to make him "clean" of his disease. "Moved with pity," Jesus touched him and willed the man to "be clean," and "immediately the leprosy left him" and the man was cleansed of his disease. After the death of Jesus, his disciples, who had few rituals or sacraments other than baptism by water and communion, would as part of their ministry place hands on others to bring comfort or give thanks. The spirit, it seems, is weak until the flesh is willing.

I believe in the transforming power of touch. The face of a lover in our hands confirms our humanity. Another's hand in mine calms me. I can't buy most of the pseudo-scientific explanations of this power, especially "touch therapy" which holds that the balance in fields of energy around our bodies can be restored by the touch of a trained therapist. The inventor of this particular form of charlatanism was a theosophist named Dolores Krieger who relied heavily on language about energy fields from quantum physics, but some of the scientific lingo is taken out of context and other phrases, such as the exchange of "qualities of energy," are suspect. Studies by scientists offer no evidence that touch therapy works.

But touching does. Who would deny this? My wife worked for a while in an elementary school in a poor rural area of North Carolina. Every afternoon when she came home from work her clothes were disheveled and she looked worn down, as if she had been carrying heavy packages for miles. From the beginning of the school day to the end her students held her hand or pulled her blouse or played with her hair. By the end of the year, she felt like a Teddy bear with all the fur rubbed off. The kids, she said, are hungry for human touch.

When my dad was dying, he was confined to a hospital bed, and I would hold his hand. We had never been particularly physical in our affections before that, but he wanted to hold my hand. We talked. We watched TV. All the while he held my hand. At times, when I thought he was sleeping, I would rise to go, and he would grip my hand hard. "Stay here," he said. So, we sat, mostly in silence, with me holding his hand while eternity closed in on him from all sides. I feel it now as I type, his grip on my fingers, a kind of afterimage for the hand, though he has been dead many years, his absence made palpable. Perhaps that is the point.

Last year my daughter Alice took confirmation vows with the Methodist church, and her mother and I stood behind her as her sponsor. Others were confirmed that day, about ten in all I guess, and their proud parents stood with us. At one point the minister asked us to put our hands on our child's shoulders or head. Since grandparents and aunts and uncles were among us, the crowd at the alter rail was large so she said that if we could not put our hands directly on our children to put them on the shoulders of the person in front of us. I put my hands on my daughter and felt someone behind me put a hand on my shoulder. The service lasted only a few minutes. Words, which I don't recall now, were spoken. We said the Lord 's Prayer in unison, but the rest is a blur. What I do remember was the crowd of us—a banker, a teacher, a U.S. Senator, a nurse—so different in the course of our lives connected for a moment by our touch. Even I, an interloper on this scene, felt, as the minister liked to say, "lifted up" by the hands of others.

~ ~ ~

The universe has no other hands as far as I know. Sometimes when Madge, our dog, watches me pick a pretzel out of a bag, my wife vocalizes her canine thoughts: "Oh, Lord, for opposable thumbs!" So I wonder, if whales are as intelligent as some scientists claim, what George thought of the human hand. Had George heard songs in the ocean nursery warning against humans? What fears did our hands on his hide raise? And how much of that fear was allayed when the hands moved gently, bringing the kind of solace that only hands can?

My doctor has wonderful hands. When two of his patients meet and talk about him, they invariably comment on his comforting touch. When he faces me and places the hands along the back of my neck all of my muscles immediately relax, my body feels suddenly suspended as if in buoyant water, and when he touches my forearms or chest any tightening just disappears. Of course, hands can rip and tear and destroy. I know a man whose hands are like two slabs of meat, and he can use them as weapons. But in the end destruction seems contrary to the subtle rotary capabilities of thumbs and the fine movements of fingers. Think of any simple act of the hands, popping open a beer, for instance, and consider the myriad muscle movements involved. The strength of bone, the flexibility of tendons, and the softness and toughness of flesh are all brought to bear on the aluminum tab.

Most of our taboos involve touch. Touch this stone, this sign, this hair and tremendous energy for good or ill fills the room. Ring this doorbell and an entirely new future opens before you. Why is touch the focus of these archetypal warnings? I suspect that the delicacy of the hand invites the idea. It is at the fingertips that the bulk of our body culminates in the tenderest motions. We throw our weight around, toss elbows, and stand our ground but when we want to see an object for what it really is we cradle it in our palm or lift it to our eyes held only by the fingertips. It is that delicacy of motion that defines the hand. When we are powerless to change the world by brute strength it is the fingertip, our weakest link to it, that taps on energy lying dormant beyond us.

In the mountains where I live the grand musical tradition was transmitted by people watching each other's hands. Hedy West, the singer who gave us "500 Miles," used to visit her grandmother in my town, Blairsville, Georgia, and learned to play the banjo by watching the old woman's hand motion. That's the mountain way. The hands of old-time players are lovely to watch because they seem to produce so much sound with so little effort. You have to train the muscles you don't use to relax; that is the way one musician put it. You can't think about it, he said. You have to watch and do. The hand will teach you what you need to know. I, too, learned banjo by watching hands and once even apologized to the husband of a musician for staring so hard at his wife. I was watching her hands, I explained lamely. He seemed to understand.

"They *are* beautiful," he said with a smile.

Curiosity may have called a bunch of vacationers to the dying whale at the water's edge that morning at St. George, but some quality far more profound than that led us into the water and kept us there as the day dragged on. Some of us hesitated—I know I did—but we got in anyway, compassion overcoming inconvenience and fear as we followed our hands into the water and placed them on a suffering beast.

~ ~ ~

After our vacation was over and we had settled back to work, Louisa, whose office is next to mine, had exciting news. George was still alive! She found his story on the Clearwater Marine Aquarium internet site. We had seen the crew from the aquarium lift George from the beach with a crane and set him in a large truck for the three-hour trip. Online we learned that the whale weighed 1,000 pounds when it arrived on August 9 and had large, infected wounds in its left tail fluke. The aquarium team lowered George into a standing pool, but the whale seemed listless, could not swim, and had to be suspended in a stretcher held in place by volunteers. They did not expect it to live.

Slowly, though, George began to revive and Louisa and I followed the story on our computers. He drank formula at a rate of five gallons a day and after two weeks had gained 115 pounds. His formula consisted of milk matrix, esbilac, salt, sunflower oil, and vitamins blended together and served in gallon milk jugs at a cost of about $100 a day. By August 30 he could swim "like a champ." One of the volunteers said "that at times there was an actual wake behind him with whitecaps!" The enthusiasm of the Clearwater team filled us with excitement too. "WOW!" they wrote after this initial swim. "What a great day! We expect him to be very hungry after expending all this energy."

The *Today* show did a segment—"The lights and cameras didn't bother George"—and he was drinking up to nine gallons of formula per day by August 25. "His will to live has surprised us all," the team leader said on September 10, "and made us actually think he just might make it." Over the course of his stay at the Marina he gained more than two hundred pounds, and as late as August 18 George was still showing signs of progress. "It is so nice to see George moving around a little more." George began to talk to his volunteers. When they would prepare the stretcher in order to weigh him, he made a distinctive clicking: "we have come to call the sound 'stretcher noise.'" George was still very sick, though, and in September began to weaken. "Lymphatic swelling at the lower end of his gastro-intestinal tract" led to difficulty in digesting food and the infection from his wounds began to worsen. Around midnight of September 21, 2001, George died. He had spent 43 days under treatment and was "the longest-lived sperm whale in captivity." On the internet site the leader of the Clearwater team mentioned that scientists would be able to use the information gathered on George to help whales in the future, but added "I am equally impressed with the impact George had on us. He brought out the best in all of us."

All of us had a hand in it.

The curve of our fingers serves as a reminder.

11. Blood Mountain

From this I reach what I might call a philosophy, at any rate it is a constant idea of mine; that behind the cotton wool is hidden a pattern, that we—I mean all human beings—are connected with this; that the whole world is a work of art; that we are parts of the work of art. *Hamlet* or a Beethoven quartet is the truth about this vast mass that we call the world. But there is no Shakespeare, there is no Beethoven, certainly and emphatically there is no God; we are the words; we are the music; we are the thing itself.

—Virginia Woolf, "A Sketch of the Past"

Blood Mountain

Standing on the stone ledge of Blood Mountain, I have to check a foolish impulse to fly. I put my hand to my eyes, surveying a blue that looks pristine simply because it hangs above a horizon line that is so far away, and see a blanket of treetops a half mile below spread in lumpy folds to a misty horizon, promising me a safe landing somewhere in Tennessee. I inch closer to the edge and plant my feet, drawn by the power of the panorama and buoyed by an unearthly feeling of calm. The urge to spread my arms, lean into that emptiness, and yield to infinity is hard to resist.

Just a step, I think. It would be easy.

"Go to the mountain top & cry for a vision," an ancient Sioux poem says. Blood Mountain is a place where that can happen. It looms above the Dahlonega Plateau, forming one of the last great peaks at the southern tip of the Appalachian chain where mountains give way to the wide, flat expanse of coastal plains. The poet Byron Reece, who grew up near here, liked to lean his "elbows on the sky" that the mountain delivered to him daily and contemplate life. A convenient guardian spirit of the place, Reece farmed a field in the mountain's shadow, the surrounding peaks marking off what he knew of the holy. "My heart is native to the sky," he wrote, thinking about the hilltops of his home. "I feel," he added, the "wide sky entering my heart."

And that is how I feel as I hover at the tip of all I know about the here and now, perched on the rocky outcropping at the edge of forever, the wide sky entering my heart.

I hold my breath and close my eyes. Oh, yes. I *want* this.

~ ~ ~

The long path to this mountain precipice began at Walasi-Yi, one of the last outposts on the Appalachian trail, the path winding uphill through hardwoods. My older boy, Matt, and I have hiked it several times, and once, when he was seventeen and his brother, Sam, about ten, the three of us walked it together, one of those events that sinks a spike deep in the shifting sands between fathers and sons. When we drove from our house to the trailhead that day, we rarely saw Blood Mountain itself, even when we were right up on it. Unlike Brasstown Bald, the tallest peak in Georgia which stays in view along much of the highway, Blood Mountain remains hidden shyly behind a ridgeline of smaller hills that hug up to it. The tallest peak on the Georgia portion of the Appalachian trail, it is formidable, if for nothing else than its history. According to legend, Creek and the Cherokee battled here, the blood of the dead making the streams run red, consecrating the place and giving the mountain its name.

Starting at the marker dedicated to Reece, my boys and I headed deep into the woods, the path winding wide and flat through thickets of laurel and rhododendron. When we crossed a stream and began our ascent, the path narrowed into a sequence of switchback trails that, clearly visible in winter, stitched their way up the mountainside. At no point could we see the mountain top, our vision obscured by the canopy of tree limbs, but I could feel our upward movement in the tug of gravity on my legs and back. The universe was calling.

I answered with heavy breathing.

My sons didn't seem tired at all. They hopped from rock to rock, leapt small streams, dashed ahead and waited, laughing and talking. I paced myself. My eyes wearied of verticals as we trudged an uphill trail surrounded by a hardwood forest of oak, poplar, and hickory stretching ahead like an endless series of mirrored images, vertical lines as far as I could see. A disorienting monotony sunk in as my universe shrunk to the narrow path, the rhythm of my footsteps, and the rasp of my breath. But when we crested the foothill, our walk along the ridgeline relaxed into a saunter, my legs happy for the flat path, and I longed for an overlook so that we could see what we had left behind.

~ ~ ~

Eventually we found one. My boys and I stepped onto the enormous rock slabs near the summit of Blood Mountain, and I walked to the ledge where I had my vision. Crows flew below me, and a small Cessna buzzed into the distance at eye level. A hawk cut a lazy circle overhead, dragging a flittering shadow across the treetops. Fly—yes, it looked so easy. I saw the universe spread before me, not just mountains and streams and a blanket of trees, but the whole mighty thing, and even when I reached my hand out tentatively to break the plane of this apparition of infinite depth, I could not put the vision in perspective. The lesser hills seemed to emanate from me, the topography of the land wrenched into submission like a supplicant at my feet by a grand *trompe l'oeil,* even though I knew that the view was not created for my eye. I was created for it. I stood on the porch of the earth, and holiness held me. Sun and moon paused high above a world lit as far as I could see.

Only when Matt shouted "Hey Dad, it's over here," his voice the call of the familiar, did I step back and, reluctantly, turn away.

Matt had found the trail and was waving us on, but as we picked our way through boulders and gnarled, wind-stunted pines along the last stretch of path, my mind still clung to the ledge. What is the pull of holiness? No God had spoken to me, of that I'm sure. When I stood at the brink of a hundred-mile view, tracing the light blue humps of hills in the distance, I did not see the hem of God's sleeve in the ridgeline and imagine, in the spume of clouds gathered in the sky, his face leaning benevolently my way, and if I had I would have dismissed it as an illusion of my own making. But clearly, I felt *something*.

~ ~ ~

The word "holy" offers a clue. It shares the ancient root word *kailo* with the word "health" as well as a host of words we associate with well-being: "wholesome," "heal," "hallow" (as in bless) and "wassail" (as in *cheers!*). In its most ancient form "holy" meant uninjured in the sense of complete. Until we are in a holy state our lives feel fractured and undone, but in the state of holiness we feel whole and no longer yearn for completion.

I envy those who can feel a deity's love in such moments. St. John of the Cross wrote that on "one dark night" when "fired by love's urgent longing" he left his quiet house, his only light being "the one that burned" in his heart. With the sky moonless and the path dark, the glow within lit the way, a guiding light he called it, more lovely than the dawn. Eventually the radiance led to God—"Him I knew so well"—who appeared as a lover waiting at the end of the path. "I abandoned and forgot myself," he wrote, as he kissed his "Beloved" and lay his head on God's breast. Gender no longer mattered and his old sense of himself was suddenly shattered. At that moment, "all things ceased," he wrote, and "I went out from myself."

All things ceased, yes, but who would *not* trade all he had to brush up against the lips of God?

St. Teresa, a friend of John of the Cross, suffered the stabbing pains of Christ's lance at her breast. Sometimes in her visions Jesus wore a crown of thorns and showed her his wounds, and once he took her rosary into his hands and recast the stones into diamonds that no one else could see. Her visions of Christ flashed so vividly before her eyes that she feared they might be from the devil, and when she explained what she saw to her superiors they agreed, and chastised her. At their request, she snapped her fingers in the face of the next apparition of Christ, trying to make the sight go away. It did not work. Jesus spoke to her and gazed at her with sublime sympathy. Afterward she could not put what she saw into words—she could not tell the color of those eyes—but she knew they watched her lovingly. The look, the divine gaze, was real and, eventually, she came to the conclusion that these visions could not be illusions.

Who, I wonder, would not gladly suffer steel under the flesh to see the colorless all color of the eyes of God?

There was a time in human history when God spoke to everyone. The primitive mind made little separation between itself and the rest of the universe. Much of the lives of the ancients was spent, as the Aboriginals put it, in "The Dreaming." Able to set aside consciousness, they passed through the world the way we do through dreams, each object animated in a way that we, who understand history and are adept with language and science, cannot imagine. In this state their lives unfolded, as the lives of animals do I suppose, with little intention. It is not that trees spoke to them or the wind whispered any more than trees speak to us in our dreams. Rather, they *were* the trees and the wind, in much the same way that all the characters in our dreams are actually us in disguise.

A vestige of this dream state clings like trailing clouds of glory to our purest religious mystics. Jesus learned God's will at Gethsemane. Sioux cries for divine visions were answered. Allah delivered the Koran to Muhammad. Moses did hear the voice of God in the burning bush, of that I am convinced. I believe these holy scriptures. Modern minds, by trance or intoxicants or flagellation or fasting—by myriad devices to transform consciousness—can hear God as well. The exhausted can hear God. The desperate and zealous can hear God. Even the insane can hear God.

But I can't.

~ ~ ~

At the top of Blood Mountain, a stone sanctuary lies nestled among enormous slabs of rock that rise, cantilevered, out of the mountain's summit. Built by the Civilian Conservation Corps in the 1930's, it shelters hikers who need a resting place along the trail. Ever since my first trip up the mountain, the stone cabin has held some inexplicable allure for me. Now that I was past the precipice, it stood squat before me like the answer to some question I had been trying to formulate. My boys and I looked through the rough window openings and saw a fireplace against the wall, a small broom, some firewood off to the side, and a doorway to a back room. During a sudden blizzard here in the eighties, we heard stories about hikers who weathered the storm in the cabin until a helicopter crew could rescue them, and, I realized, looking inside, what a blessed haven this must have been for someone buried deep in snow.

The boys lost interest in the drab stone interior and ran off to leap the high rocks, but long after they went their way I kept looking. Shafts of light, sprinkled with dust, cut heavy triangles into the stony space, carving out several shades of ochre in the darkness. Light puddled on the middle of the floor revealing ridges and textures in the stone, but the corners remained hidden in shadows. Yes, if God could visit me, this stone cabin would be the place.

What if I told the boys to go back without me, and I spent the night here alone? Would God visit me in this chamber? What would he look like? The gash of a sunbeam would cross the floor, I suppose, and glow briefly on the far wall while the shadows of broom handle and firewood grew long and faded in the soft light. Later, as I huddled in a corner, awaiting the divine presence, the darkness in the room would spread like an oily puddle, filling the cabin. Wind would whip through the rocks offering a sad, inhuman moan. A rat might scuttle along the far wall and squeal. Would God call my name? Would the Beloved appear in the cold to warm me? Would the eyes of God look down on me with loving sympathy? When God visited the cabin, would he stand regally before me, his countenance shining, or would he come dressed in nighttime and cover his eyes behind a cloak of spectral moonlight?

Turning away from the cabin, I felt incomplete and yearned for that kiss against my cheek. I saw bright blue above the thrusted rocks and wanted to gorge myself on the sky.

~ ~ ~

The boys and I looked around a bit, tossed a few stones into the vast open scenery about us, and decided to head back down the mountain before darkness fell. Along the way we came across the stone ledge again, my launching pad into holiness, the rock slab facing now on a dusky sky. The sun hung low, and I knew that we had to get down the hill in a hurry, but I paused anyway. No longer tempted to fly, I felt instead the planet's slow turn, as its enormous penumbral shadows spread over the land, and I imagined what this scene must look like at night when the darkness above filled with a spray of stars.

It was time to go home.

That night long after the family had gone to sleep, I walked out on the porch of my house and thought about my moment at the precipice. Now safely at home and surrounded by the familiar, I stepped out from under the porch to look at the stars, but a mist had fallen over the valley obscuring the sky. So, I closed my eyes, imagining myself again on the precipice but at night this time, a map of the night sky forming above me, marked off with those familiar dotted line-drawings of godlike heroes including Orion, Cassiopeia, and the Twins enshrined in the zodiac and gliding eternally through the Milky Way. Why do we fill the empty spaces with pictures of ourselves? Why do we hunt for a familiar face in the stars? What would happen if I erased the lines?

In the end, I did not spend the night in a mountain sanctuary isolated from those I love. My wife slept beside me as usual in our warm and comfortable bed. For now, at least, I live my life in the valley enveloped in work and job and family. I harvest my own tomatoes and grade my exams. When my son calls my name, I turn to him and cannot imagine a day that I wouldn't. I am no saint, to be sure. I keep my elbows planted firmly on the porch rail and leave heaven to others. It is the universe I feel on my cheek, not a kiss. But the hike offered a moment of Aboriginal dreaminess, a glimpse of a reality on the mountain top that cannot be dismissed with the snap of the fingers. It was a crazy impulse to fly, but I can return to it any time that I close my eyes, look hard at holiness walking toward me dressed as the night sky, and, yielding to infinity at last, disconnect the dots.

Orphaned Souls

This year I gave up an office with a window for one with a closet, and, despite Romantic misgivings, I think I got the better end of the deal. Facing a wall six feet away, my old office did not have much of a view. I took solace from the symmetry of brick, but the window did not yield much light. The windowsill sat at ground level, so I occasionally had the experience, while reading, of watching a lawn mower pass within a few feet of my nose, the room roaring and shaking like an airplane hangar. A favorite student pasted the decal of a crescent moon on the windowpane to cheer me, but as the years went by, the decal curled at the edges and waned forlorn on the glass reminding me of students long gone. In my new office I miss looking out but the view from that window, perpetually cast in shadow, always seemed a little gloomy like an endless string of rainy days.

A closet, on the other hand, now that's a gift. A hidden chamber! What professor of literature could resist? Before its reincarnation, my closet belonged to the entire English department, but now it exists solely for my pleasure. I can easily step into it and admire tiers of shelves rising in Dantean layers to the ceiling, empty of all sins but my own. Unlike the office itself, which displays diplomas and books, the closet is the business end of the operation where glossy and metallic supplies wait, like the Swiss Guard, ready to impose order on chaos. Of course, my closet doesn't have a view either—no pastoral nonsense allowed in here—but it does have a light so when the door is left ajar a comforting glow spills from the little recess like the nimbus of a cloister.

The word "closet" may be wrong. There is no dowel for hanging sweaters and coats, and I wouldn't dream of putting clothes in it. No, this is the inner sanctum. Here, amid staplers, scissors, Wite-Out, and the other necessary sundries of my holy of holies, I keep at eye level the books I am teaching. *Beowulf* holds the position of honor this week. Each night, I set the text in its nest of ungraded papers where the tome awaits my return, gnawing on the absolute dark that only a closet in a windowless office can provide, nurtured on enclosure and growing stronger in the inky black.

I had no misgivings about the new space—the change, my colleagues agreed, looking about with hands in pockets and nodding at my good fortune, was for the better. Then one morning the power went out. I had just gone to the closet to get my text for class when the office was plunged into darkness, and I stood unable to move, the book useless in my hand. I waited for my eyes to grow accustomed to the dark, but there were no shades of gray in this compact blackness for my eyes to adjust to. Slowly I became aware of myself as the sole presence in the gloom. I heard my own breathing as if for the first time, and, when I raised my hand in front of my eyes and wiggled the fingers, seeing nothing, I felt the heavy helplessness of my invisible presence. In a moment or two, the lights flickered, the computer whirred, snapped, and bleeped back to life, and the closet reclaimed its comforting glow. But for the length of that black spell, I was suddenly and completely alone.

The philosopher William James wrote about the wonder of such an ordinary experience. "Shut oneself in a closet," he explained, and "begin to think of the fact of one's being there, of one's queer bodily shape in the darkness, of one's fantastic character." It is true, that is part of what I felt.

The body that was so familiar to me in daytime immediately became a fantastic creature, a presence I felt but could not see, *my* shape made suddenly strange. I thought of Seamus Heaney's description of Grendel, Beowulf's bestial foe, as a "dog's breath in the dark." For William James such a moment can bring us to the wonder of mere existence. "Not only that anything exists," he writes, "but that this very thing should be, is mysterious." With the familiar props pulled away we are allowed to experience the wonder of merely being *this* being, and I did.

But as the amazing fact of my simply being presented itself in that dark, another equally potent realization swept over me, brought on, perhaps, by my wonder at the oddity of my creation. I felt totally alone. With my own body swept aside as some thing of darkness that did not belong to me, my consciousness of that fact was all that I had left. It, my own consciousness, alone remained familiar to me in the coffin-like closeness. Grendel had his mother in their murky lair, but I had only my awareness of my own peculiarity as I clutched the useless book and clipboard firmly to my body. In the dark, I felt orphaned in the world.

~ ~ ~

Despite grappling with his own demons in the dark, William James generally had a sunny view of life. According to his sister he delighted in his country house with "fourteen doors, all opening outwards." A psychologist as well as a philosopher, James was the one who argued that consciousness was not some ghostly entity of the mind, but a stream, the famous "stream of consciousness" that flows like a daily miracle through the lives of each of us. Through this consciousness the mind creates reality not by making it up whole cloth but by drawing its attention to objects and thoughts and memories. Whatever the conscious mind focuses on becomes most real, the center-stream flood of our attention, while the rest of experience foams and splatters at the periphery, losing its grip on us as it glimmers on the edge of our awareness. So, consciousness is ever shifting, flowing, with new objects and thoughts and memories bobbing into focus as we turn our attention in new directions. Jacques Barzun, in his lovely homage, *A Stroll with William James*, writes that "James himself never ceased to marvel at its character," calling it "the wonderful stream of our consciousness." It is the glittering surge of our days.

This home-grown and purely American philosophy rang true to me when I first came across it in the little paperback book, *Pragmatism and Other Essays* and has stuck with me since. His metaphor of consciousness as a stream aptly describes the wayward and contradictory nature of thought that Montaigne discovered when he wrote. "My judgment does not always go forward. It floats, it strays." It drifts, he explained, like "a tiny boat." All of those fluid tropes for consciousness describe my mind as well, and go a long way toward explaining why I am an essayist. Reading James made me feel at ease with the way the world occurred to me. It opened all of the doors of my mind, happily outward.

But there is one way that James' view of the mind differs from my own, and I came to it most forcibly in the darkness of that office. He believed that if God could be found anywhere, it was at the twilight edge where the attention of consciousness flickers and fades into the region of the mind beyond consciousness. It is at the spumy shore of consciousness that we sense "something more," he wrote in *The Varieties of Religious Experience*, "operative outside the conscious self, continuous with it and *of the same quality*." Not only is God out there, this line of reasoning suggests, he is like us and related to us.

James was never sure about God. "He did not really believe," his contemporary George Santayana said. "He merely believed in the right of believing that you may be right if you believed." That's not much of a credo, and it does sound like James who was wary of any kind of transcendent reality. But even though he may have been skeptical about God's existence, he did argue that we were never completely by ourselves in the universe either. Walk into a closet, shut the door, and turn off the lights. Separate yourself entirely from others in the world and, James claimed, you still have a direct line to "something more…outside the conscious self…but continuous with it." For James, the world completes us, and that is why he embraced it with open doors.

~ ~ ~

Unlike James, I believe we are orphaned souls. Almighty forces are at work in the universe governed by laws that rule down to the puzzling properties of the tiniest subatomic particle, but they don't care a quark about us. They may have given birth to us, but they abandoned us on the doorstep of an enormous nothingness that extends at least as far as the eye can see. This is my article of faithlessness. So, when I am alone in a black closet, I am utterly alone. I may marvel at the unique creation there in that particular dark, but I don't have company. When I step out under a night sky or face the ocean or hear the wind moaning in the hills above me, I sense something more in the universe, something much more, but I know it is something other. I have never felt the sense that my consciousness connects to God.

And I'm not about to slip God in through my peripheral vision either. If James believed that God glitters in the twilight space between our conscious and unconscious minds, then he is engaging in wishful thinking.

He was, after all, a kind man who flirted with the idea that wishing made it so. But if God is in the unconscious mind—that free-floating mental stuff at the subliminal edges of consciousness, available to us in our dreams— then a personal God is not a being separate from our own but, quite literally, a figment of our imagination, and we are still alone. When God speaks to our hearts, it is *our* hearts speaking. Our dreams may delight and illuminate us; they may fuel the songs and stories and plays that we use to comfort each other in the dark closets of our nights, and they may, as well, fill us with fears, but they are the nightly whimperings of an orphan.

~   ~   ~

Literature, I tell my students on the first day of class, is a lullaby to our orphaned souls. Perhaps that's why so many orphans from Oedipus to Pip to Harry Potter wander through the pages of our books. Like abandoned children huddled around a bedtime voice, my students bring their various consciousnesses to bear on the ancient texts that we read aloud together. Most days they wear outwardly the nonchalance of youth—the dark-haired young man with hair falling casually over his brow and searing, dreamy eyes slouching at the back of the room, the chubby one with long blonde hair sitting upright with rounded shoulders, sad eyes, and a tight smile, or the young woman in a turban with olive skin, dark eyebrows, and onyx eyes full of mystery and wonder—but I know that many of my bright-faced students also carry burdens, confessing in my office that they cut themselves, can't sleep, have lost their faith, drink too much, are lonely and abused—the gamut of youthful woes that I have heard over the years.

"A ring-whorled prow rode into the harbor, ice-clad, outbound," I recite slowly standing before them. This is the moment in the opening pages of *Beowulf* when the Danes set the body of their lord, Shield, on a funeral boat piled with "far-fetched treasures" and cast the boat laden with "battle tackle," "bladed weapons," and "coats of mail" onto the wide waters of death with little more than the hope of a vaguely understood afterlife. Above the boat, they raise a flag and watch the body of the old king carried off "to wind and tide" amid the wails of his people. "No man," the voice of the ancient text tells us, "knows for certain who salvaged that load."

When I read aloud to the students, I feel the power of shared words to bring balm. I know this is true because I was once one of them. I remember vividly—so vividly I could reach out and feel the chill—one cold, September morning, dragging my scraggly young self across the Wake Forest College campus after a sleepless night full of troubling questions, to hear Professor Edwin Wilson, the man who taught me to love literature, read from William Wordsworth's "The Prelude" and learning that whatever I was feeling had been felt before. Literature frames our otherwise unutterable fears, giving them voice, and by speaking them we know that we have each other and are not alone with our burdens. Occasionally in the orphanage of my classes a student in the back row will fall asleep—this is a lullaby after all—but most of them listen hard and take in the words, and some, I know because I am still one of them, hear the unuttered questions that they haul about with them daily spoken aloud in a room lined with bright windows, absorbing enough comfort to get through the black closet of another night.

Literature has long done this job, comforting those who will listen even when God has abandoned them. In the pagan world of *Beowulf,* the bard sings a song about the rescue of a queen to calm the nerves of warriors who had just faced, and destroyed, a hideous monster. While he sings, a "pleasant murmur" rises among warriors struggling with memories of dead comrades. Under the spell of song, they sit on benches and recline toward one another, even those who had feuded in the past, the music creating a momentary camaraderie among them. The queen, Wealhtheow, who has been serving mead, hears the familiar tune about the plight of a woman in her position, and sits among her men for a while. She pours a drink for the new hero, Beowulf, and sends it up the table to him, the goblet passing from hand to hand. Later she will return to her accustomed place, apart from the men, but for now she shares a song with her protectors and enjoys their company. The bard may sing harp tunes to please the prince who had killed the beast, but he brings comfort to all in earshot, including, of course, us.

We may be alone in the universe, but at least we have each other. That is the ultimate lesson of our poetry. When I ask a tough question in class and my students look at me with puzzled faces, I tell them to look in the book. The book is your friend in this class. In its pages we know that our darkest fear—the black, unmentionable fear that we live in a universe that does not know what the hell we are talking about—is not ours alone. The book does not supply the answer; it *is* the answer. Others before us have set the boat of their puny lives adrift on vast, godless waters uncertain of their destination. Others before us have hung a head on the arm of a friend. Others before us cried out in the pitch black of our dark closet.

~ ~ ~

On September 11, 2001, I was sitting in my office preparing the last pages of *Beowulf* when the awful news arrived. I heard colleagues speaking anxiously outside my door, though I could not make out what they were saying, and I heard one storm out of the building declaring he was going home. For some reason I sat in my office, staring at the book, preferring for a while not to know. Later that morning I stood with several students in the Student Center and watched on television as a plane crashed into the second tower of the World Trade Center. We saw the skyscrapers fall as terrified New Yorkers with handkerchiefs over their mouths fled from an avalanche of smoke that engulfed the city's streets, and we heard commentators solemnly intone that "everything had changed."

The next morning an e-mail from the college counselor encouraged us to discuss the terrorist attack in class as a way of easing anxiety among the students, so I read the funeral scene from *Beowulf* aloud to my students and we talked.

The funeral begins with Beowulf's people gathering wood for the pyre and piling it carefully on the high ground until the structure "stood four square." Before his death, Beowulf had asked his comrades to drape the timbers with weapons which they did, setting their dead hero in the middle of the stack, weeping and mourning all the while. When they lit the tinder, dark smoke quickly enveloped the body and Beowulf's people cried out, but soon the flames roared so that none of their cries could be heard and the weeping became a tableau of silent anguish as the body fell away from the skeleton and flames "wrought havoc in the hot bone house, burning it to the core." With the king dead, the people felt suddenly exposed and vulnerable. Enemy Swedes, we are told, were gathering ominously on the horizon, watching for their moment to strike, and one woman, feeling a sense of foreboding and catching a glimpse of a dreadful future, fell away from the crowd, bewailing her fate. Husbands will be killed, she screamed, and women raped in front of their children and dragged by their hair into slavery. "Heaven," the Christian monk who edited the text felt compelled to add, "swallowed up the smoke."

Seamus Heaney, who gave us this striking translation of the Anglo-Saxon poem, wrote about the scene. "The Geat woman who cries out in dread as the flames consume the body of the dead lord could come straight from a late twentieth century news report, from Rwanda or Kosovo," Heaney wrote before 9/11, and "her keen is a nightmare glimpse into the minds of people who have survived traumatic, even monstrous events who are now being exposed to a comfortless future." I had written his comment on the board for the students on 9/12, and as we talked it became clear, without anyone saying so, that our country had now been added to that list of traumatized countries.

After class, a student hung back to speak while I was packing up my books. Her friendly round face almost always wore a smile, but today she looked a little worn down. This was the first class that the teacher did not mention the terrorist attack, she told me. She did not offer her comment as a criticism, but more as a relief. After she left, I wished that I had had the presence of mind to tell her she was wrong. Beowulf's funeral pyre—the wooden tiers crashing in on a gush of flames, sending plumes of black smoke into the sky—*was* 9/11 for the ancient Danes. The towering gables of Heorot Hall, the great mead palace of king Hrothgar which was the center of the Danish universe, would soon go up in flames in "a barbarous burning," and the old order that seemed impregnable would come tumbling down. The woman keening at the base of the roaring pyre wails for herself, her children, and her people, and, in a book that grows stronger in the dark, she wails for us.

THE RAZOR BLADE

My favorite book is a battered, cloth-bound American Heritage Dictionary from the 1970's. It came to me from my father, who picked it up as part of a promotional campaign when he worked with the Animal Feeds Division of American Cyanamid, a pharmaceutical company. Like the old—very old—Webster's unabridged that sits on a circular table in the English department offices where I work, the edges of its pages have turned a mottled, thrush brown from the oil of thumbs that they have for years fluttered beneath, but unlike that boxy tome, the American Heritage is broad and tall—when opened, it fills up the desktop—and is, well, more handsome, though the bent covers of both books, rubbed raw at the corners like the worn cuffs of an aristocrat strapped for cash, have the same tattered elegance about them.

Most dictionaries include etymologies that trace words back to Greek, Roman, and other ancient sources, but the AHD goes further, and deeper, into the history of the language by offering the Indo-European sources of the words as well, tracing language back more than five-thousand years along the circuitous route of shifting sounds—vowel transformations and consonant substitutions—that mark the wars, famines, pillaging, forced migrations, and genocides that brought these words, honed by the ravages of time, to my lips and this page, the AHD taking us way back to a time when the word for poetry and the word for a marker of piled stones were one in the same.

Not long ago I thought that I had lost this dear, old book and nearly fell into despair. I had been doing my writing in my office, not at home, and in the course of moving misplaced it. I accused my wife, Barbara, who had complained about its badly worn appearance, of discarding the dictionary, but she secretly loves the old book, too, and insisted that she hadn't and later produced it for me hidden among some papers in my old study. It *is* in pretty bad shape. The cover is completely ripped away from its binding and the title page, jammed between the worn boards, is wrinkled in hundreds of accordion folds. It is out of date, with almost none of the new cyber-lingo of the computer world in it, words I can, apparently, live without. As a final blow, the tops of the last few pages have been unceremoniously ripped away so that certain root words in the w's have been, in my office at least, consigned to an early oblivion.

And yet, I would not discard this book, in part because it came from my dad, and in part because the oils that have stained its pages are largely mine. A book marker, with the word "copse" printed on it has held a shady place for me on page 294 for more than a decade, and the coffee stain under the illustration of a cutlass on page 327 was no doubt dribbled there by a younger me as well. Like rosary beads and worry stones and the communion chalice—all lovingly rubbed and cared for over time—the AHD at my elbow has acquired its sacred status by use.

~ ~ ~

Any object can become sacred which is a word not just for those objects that are holy, but for those that are *made* holy. Since its earliest definition in English, the word "sacred" has been associated with the ritual enactment of the Eucharist. It is related to words for holy activities such as "consecrate" and "obsecrate," and was easily transformed into the verb "sanctify." In the Indo-European language it was, apparently, coupled with the word for "doer," as in sak-ro-dhot, the performer of sacred rites, which gives rise to our word "sacerdotal" for priestly activities. What separates the word "sacred" from the sedentary word "holy," the language tells us, is the idea of action, and lurking there in the sounds of the word's first four letters, is, as well, another word: sacrifice. We use the word to describe the way we spend ourselves, use up our selves, in matters of the spirit.

A Royal typewriter sits on the floor of my office, another scarred object that is sacred to me. It belonged to my wife's family, purchased, a metal plate on the front says, from the Gaston Office Machine Co. in Cramerton, N.C. The look and feel of this office machine were inspired by the Sherman tank. With a heavy, army-issue metal casing and a carriage arm cocked smartly to one side in perpetual salute, it looks more martial than saintly to be sure, but it stands at the ready to conduct matters of the spirit, though in the age of computers it has been largely swept aside. Occasionally a student with a form to fill out—still an awkward procedure on the computer—will come by my office, drag the typewriter out from behind my desk, and set it up on the table in the English office, ready for action before young, consternated faces. When they try to type, sinking fingers into the keys, the consternation usually gives way to laughter as they learn the true meaning of "heavy duty." Their hands, made dainty by the soft touch of the computer keyboard, are not up to the Royal which has a keyboard with a kick and requires a pianist's sure hands. It is, after all, a *manual* typewriter, and *mano a mano* is the expected method of combat. This is a typewriter for pounding out books.

A veteran of the war of words, the Royal has certainly seen action in the past. I typed college papers on it as well as many bad poems, and several failed novels. The old tank bears dings and gouges and drips of Wite-Out as battle scars, and the words suffered into existence by the little hammers of its keys remain faintly superimposed, one upon another, in the soft and receptive surface of the black roller. I see in retrospect that the typewriter has taken the shape of my early literary career, with a vague look of defeat about its hardened exterior. After twenty years at the fingertips of a poet manqué it has become resigned to a life of occasional bureaucratic duties far from the front lines of literary skirmishes. But as I lower the typewriter back into its spot on the floor, its carriage sliding awry and bell ringing away, I know that the old tank did not lose the battles that its owner couldn't win. The aptly named Royal, that settles wherever it lands with a clunk, serves as a reminder that in battles of the spirit what counts is the attempt. Time lost in literary combat is not wasted, but sacrificed in the service of a greater glory—whether individual glory is attained or not.

~   ~   ~

All of us have, in the small of our backs, a triangular wedge of bone called the sacrum, so named because it was used by priests during sacrificial rituals. Sacred. Sacrifice. We hear the connection in the language and feel it in our bones. The word "scarred" is a near acronym for sacred which is fitting, although there is no etymological connection between the words. In addition to action, what sets the word "sacred" apart from the more benign "holy" is spilt blood. We know from the blackened but otherwise well-preserved remains of sacrificial victims found in peat bogs, that Europeans conducted sacrifices some four- or five-thousand years ago. The most famous of these is the Tollund Man, who, wearing a skullcap and holding his eyes closed shut, was hanged and thrown in the bog either as a

135

punishment or a sacrifice. Lines about the eyes and bristles of beard show clearly on the blackened face which looks remarkably serene, frozen in a final expression that it has worn for a millennium.

Sacrifice was probably woven into the entire fabric of society in the form of the "Three-Fold Death" described by J.P. Mallory in his book, *In Search of the Europeans*. Among German tribes this practice included the "punishments of hanging, stabbing and drowning, each technique correlated to the crime for which the victim was convicted." In 1951 the body of a young girl who had been sacrificed in the first century AD was pulled from the peat bogs. The malnourished girl had been blindfolded, her head partially shaved. It is not clear how she had been killed. There were no signs of strangulation on her neck, but the body had been weighted down with birch branches and a large stone to keep it under the surface of the bog. This child's death was punishment, not sacrifice. She was probably an adulteress. Tacitus, the Roman historian, wrote that the Germanic people often shaved the heads of adulteresses. But whether it is punishment or sacrifice it follows the same pattern—the same ritual—and the enormity of killing one so young for such a crime makes her the victim.

We are drawn to such horrors. There is—upon hearing this description and seeing photographs—an undeniable, voyeuristic urge to know who we are by knowing who these people were. Seamus Heaney, the Irish poet, read the struggles of his country into the image of the "poor scapegoat" and wrote a sequence of poems based on these ancient, Germanic sacrifices.

So, who are we?

I see in memory a student, hair soaked from the rain, who has come to my office with an awful gift, and I know.

~   ~   ~

Hidden under pens and pencils in a cup on my desk is one of my most sacred possessions. It is a razor blade. It was given to me by a student who went barefoot most days, liked to lead a procession of fellow students walking atop brick campus walls on warm nights, and went skinny dipping with friends at the base of mountain waterfalls. She was a kid—a little wild, mostly silly, I think. She was also the most verbally gifted undergraduate I have ever taught, writing fresh and striking poetry and prose as naturally, it seemed, as she skipped.

She came by the office almost every day to talk about poets and writers and words and friends. She was forever transforming herself, one day a blonde, the next a brunette with perhaps a streak of green. Some days she came to the office like a pixy or Peter Pan in cut-off jeans and some flimsy, gauzy top. But she also went through a phase when she traipsed around campus like a bag lady weighed down by heavy coats, the bells dangling from her waist clanging and clanking as she flopped down in the big green chair in my office.

Her days were filled with light and flowers and poetry, but her nights were very different, I'm afraid. Like many gifted children, she was troubled. She rarely slept well, she told me, didn't eat properly, and sometimes out of depression, cut herself. I worried about her—still do, in fact, though she has gone off to another school now—and I told her that if she ever felt pushed to the end of her endurance, if she ever felt that she could not handle her demons, she should call me, day or night, at any hour.

She never did. Instead, she brought gifts, born of her nights. She would come by the office, sometimes bleary-eyed, often looking pale and ill. "Hey Doc," she would say rifling through her book bag. "Look at this."

Sometimes it was a poem. Sometimes a book. She was ecstatic when her dad bought the collected T.S. Eliot and some books by Sylvia Plath and she spread those out for me one day. She often brought flowers, including a bouquet of dead dandelions which I kept for as long as I could stand it and then tossed out my window. She brought paintings and on one big day a special gift, a mobile made of goat horns, crescent moons, keys, bells, and the medallion from the Georgia region AA essay contest which she won in high school.

These, I know, were gifts of nights when she beat back her demons with art. Making gifts for me got her through the night, I think. The most beautiful, though, was the razor blade. One of the last times she came to my office, she fumbled through her bag as usual digging through books and papers, her bells clanging, and pulled it out. At first I did not know what it was, this blade wrapped in cardboard. But then I did see.

"This is for you," she said. "I won't be needing it anymore."

All about my office hang her other gifts: bookmarks, leaves, drawings. Her poems are stacked in a notebook on my selves. But the razor stays in a cup beside me as I write. A few nights later she left the college coming by the office and rubbing a moon decal on my window, another gift from her nights. Not long after that, dandelions began to sprout in the grass just beyond my window and spread into the rest of the yard.

To get the song we gouge out the fingerboard and to keep the poem we turn down the corner of the page. Art leaves a scar, a measure of the impact of the spirit on the world. My dictionary tears loose of its binding, the enormous stack of pages falling onto the desk with a whoosh. The typewriter, tough as it is, keeps a sacerdotal record in pentimento on the rubber roller, and a girl—okay, a young woman really, but a little spring hope—writes a poem far into the night with the razor blade just out of reach. The tears, the gouges, the dings, and the razors are reminders that we cannot assign our holiness to the air. We bear it into the world.

139

LIVING MIDNIGHT

Last night I had a bout of insomnia. It happens sometimes. I wake up. The clock strikes four. I go to the bathroom, get a drink of water, and head back to the bed, trying to lie still so that I will not wake my wife. A thought comes to me—the writer's curse—so I get up, go into the bathroom again to jot it down, and return crawling back under the covers. Consciously holding still of course only makes matters worse since I am beating back the urge to turn and toss and so lie stiffly. And what is that light? I get up again, this time to gaze at the full moon turning the world into a powdery, colorless day. That doesn't help. I shut the door, go back to bed and close my eyes to block out the moonlit glow on the window shades. I have been rereading Jean-Dominique Bauby who compares the solitude of his paralyzed body to a diving bell, and under my closed eyelids I feel myself drifting down into the depths of the ocean of self, the bell bobbing back and forth as I breathe, unable to move or speak, locked in my solitary state with nothing but doom and my failures to mull over. It takes a while. The clock strikes five.

I head downstairs to get a book.

~ ~ ~

Readers of *The Diving Bell and the Butterfly* know the solitude Bauby recreates on the page. Barely tethered to the world of others, he seems to speak to us from an echoey place far away. I'm not talking about his physical isolation which was nearly unbearable. At the age of forty-three, Bauby—an editor for *Elle* magazine—suffered a stroke that rendered all but the lid of one eye completely useless. Suddenly the witty and gregarious Parisian journalist was locked into his body with his mind intact. Once his condition was stabilized and understood, he learned to communicate through a system called partner-assisted scanning and wrote his book by composing it in his head and dictating it one letter at a time. In an agonizingly slow process, his partner read the alphabet to him over and over and he chose each letter of his story by blinking his one good eye. It is this suffocating isolation that makes his book so harrowing—and compelling—for his readers.

The feeling of isolation I'm interested in, though, is the one he creates on the page, the one that we experience with him as we read the book. It colors the entire memoir but at certain moments the distance between himself and the world thickens in a lyrical prose offering insights into the way writers of nonfiction communicate solitude by exploiting a paradox inherent in any writer's task. In one of these moments Bauby is playing a game with his son, Théophile.

> …we can certainly play hangman, the national preteen sport. I guess a letter, then another, then stumble on the third. My heart is not in the game. Grief surges over me. His face not two feet from mine, my son Théophile sits patiently waiting—and I, his father, have lost the simple right to ruffle his bristly hair, clasp his downy neck, hug his small, lithe, warm body tight against me. There are no words to express it. My condition is monstrous, iniquitous, revolting, horrible.

In many ways Bauby is not alone here in the room of this page about a hangman drawn in a guessing game. His daughter, Celeste, is with him in addition to his son, and he can communicate well enough to play the game which only requires single letter responses. In fact, a social component is built into all his days at the hospital. The staff attends to him daily, he dictates regularly to his assistant Claude Mendibil, sees other patients, and is often visited by friends and other members of his family. But these social encounters are burdened by the weight of his immobility, the "diving bell" as he calls his body. He may be able to play the game of hangman, but simple acts of affection are denied him. He tries to find abstractions for his agony in words such as "monstrous, iniquitous, revolting" and "horrible," but they don't help. All he can do to communicate his emotion now is cry, which his son notices—cry and lose the game.

What intensifies the solitude is Bauby's lyrical power to express in his memoir, what he cannot in the moment say. He cannot hug his son or ruffle his hair, but it is the language of carefree physicality in verbs such as "ruffle," "clasp," and "hug" that express how much he misses the ability to touch and hold his loved ones. Later in the passage it is the heartbreaking irony of thinking "Don't be scared, little man" and "I love you," but not being able to say the words when he needs them. And it is, of course, in the irony of his losing the game and becoming—in the stick drawing done by his son—the man sentenced to be hanged by a rope from the gallows of his wheelchair. "On a corner of the page," Bauby writes, Théophile "completes his drawing of the gallows, the rope, and the condemned man."

This expressive language—rich in action verbs, imagery, and figuration—is the butterfly of the book's title, capturing a mind free to fly to all the places his body cannot go. "You can visit the woman you love," he writes, "slide down beside her and stroke her still sleeping face." Or "build castles in Spain, steal the Golden Fleece, discover Atlantis, realize your childhood dreams and adult ambitions." Being wheeled to the patio with a view of a lighthouse or propped up in front of other patients during a social hour or smelling food being cooked—these events trigger imaginative flights that are often humorous and touching, but the language of these flights of imagination, like the words describing his affection for his son, provide relief while they accentuate his torment. Hanging onto the page of life by a string of letters he is both pathetic in abject isolation and heroic in his ability to transcend that isolation and deliver himself as a fully aware, sentient, and in the end wise bearer of his burden. He may reach out to his son—and to us—but only one letter at a time, so his solitude, where he dangles enclosed in oceanic stillness like the man in the diving bell, is intensified by the paradox of putting his isolation with great difficulty into the shared medium of words.

He is, in short, a writer.

~ ~ ~

But it is not Bauby that I need tonight as, fully awake now, I walk past the open copy on the end table by the sofa. I don't need more isolation. Downstairs, I scan the bookshelves in my study, and survey my favorites. Maybe I choose Edward Abbey. I take down his memoir *Desert Solitaire: A Season in the Wilderness,* and flip to the first pages. After driving 750 miles from Albuquerque, Abbey arrived for his ranger assignment at the Arches Monument Park in the middle of the night and climbed into his own diving bell. His job was to live alone in a tiny house trailer on this arid site and write a report once a month, his trailer an isolation chamber eerily like Bauby's diving bell. It was "built so efficiently and compactly there's hardly room for a man to breathe," he laments, like an "iron lung," equipped "with windows and venetian blinds." Dark and cold with the stars hidden behind clouds and snow falling, Abbey could not see his surroundings until morning, but the mice in the trailer were immediately happy, "scampering around with the good news that their long lean lonesome winter was over— their friend and provider had finally arrived."

I smile. A little humor helps when you can't sleep.

Like Bauby, Abbey would not be contained by a metal box, and at dawn the next morning he opens the door of his trailer on a marvelous scene: "the center of the world, earth's naval, Abbey's country, the red wasteland." Looking toward the mountains he sees the Colorado River five or six miles away, and in the other direction he takes in vast canyonlands and mesas that dwarf the tiny town of Moab. Dotting the landscape are The Arches, large rock formations chastened by wind, rain, snow, and ice over eons of time that come in a variety of shapes: "Some resemble jug handles or flying buttresses, others bridges." At a bend in the road nearby, Balanced Rock looms above him, a fifty-foot stone incongruously mounted atop an equally large rock pedestal. Standing in this "rather personal demesne," Abbey realizes that he is the "sole inhabitant, usufructuary, observer, and custodian" of 33,000 acres. When the sun rises, the "flaming globe, blazing on the pinnacles, minarets, and balanced rocks," he greets it feeling the whole of the ninety-three million miles of black void that the light crossed to reach him, and the snow of the night before slowly begins to melt.

But no, much as I love this book, Abbey does not speak to me tonight as I stand in pajamas, hair mussed up, before the wall of books— maybe a little too much sunlight for the midnight hours I'm trying to get through. So, I put Abbey back and run my fingers down the alphabet.

I'm always tempted by Annie Dillard. I open *Holy the Firm* to a bookmark on one of my favorite passages, one I have written about in the past. "One night a moth flew into the candle," it begins; I'm tempted to read aloud, but let it ring in my head instead. I hear foreboding in the unvoiced f-whispers of "flapped into the fire" and "flamed, frazzled, and fried," as the moth struggles, and inevitable doom in the staccato surprise of "caught, burnt dry, and held." In her description of the surroundings illuminated by the flare, those e-sounds—"blue sleeves," "green leaves," and "jewelweed"—cry out, implicating us in the tiny horror. Under this intense illumination on an altar set just for the writer, but offered up to me in words, the agon proceeds in verbs of contortion and imagery of obliteration: wings "vanished," legs "clawed, curled, blackened, and ceased, disappearing utterly," head "jerked in spasms, making a spattering noise," antennae "crisped and burned away," and "heaving mouth parts crackled like pistol fire."

"I must have been staring at the candle," Dillard writes lending a hypnotic, self-absorbed element. Her isolation is made more complete by an illuminated circle growing brighter and more intense as the flame from the immolated body of the moth increases, the glow marking off a dark margin, but as the ephemera of the moth's wings disappear in a "fine, foul smoke" the scene darkens again, releasing us from the incandescent body. It's over. The ordinary life of the moth is rendered irrelevant by the ordeal: "Had she been new, or old? Had she mated and laid her eggs, had she done her work?" None of that matters here as everyday concerns are left behind. The body—"a fraying, partially collapsed gold tube jammed upright in the candle's round pool"—no longer matters as well.

There is plenty of illumination and midnight here, but tonight I need something else, and of course I knew what it would be even as I went through my insomniac ritual of checking out a few lyrical passages from my favorites first.

~   ~   ~

John Stuart Mill claimed a unique status for lyric poetry among the literary genres by arguing that while "eloquence" of other forms of writing "is *heard,* poetry is *overheard.*" Mill's goal was to distinguish between lyric poetry and the popular ballads and broadsides of the day aimed at a political audience, writing in *What is Poetry?* that "the peculiarity of poetry appears to us to lie in the poet's utter unconsciousness of a listener." He compared the lyric poem to the "lament of a prisoner in a solitary cell, ourselves listening, unseen, in the next," and defined lyric poetry as "feeling confessing itself to itself, in moments of solitude." These ideas were given further heft in the twentieth century when the critic Northrop Frye in *The Anatomy of Criticism* echoed Mill's notion that the poet "turns his back on his listeners."

Writers of essays and memoirs retreat in a similar way when their prose turns lyrical and inward, but the bond between reader and writer seems stronger than eavesdropping, causing me to question the notion of lyric as writing overheard by an unaddressed reader. While reading Bauby, I too wear his diving bell sharing in the claustrophobic quality of each word he ekes out. With Abbey I blink in the bright glow of the landscape, and when I read Dillard I feel, through the moth in flames, the sacrificial nature of art and life. We do more than listen in surreptitiously. After all, the writer's fate is not what is at stake when we read. *Ours* is.

The critic Helen Vendler in her "Introduction to *The Art of Shakespeare's Sonnets*" catches the experience precisely: the lyric voice is "an utterance for us to utter as ours." Lyric prose like that found in the books I skimmed at my bookshelves may be the product of "a mind alone with itself" but the reader is not a "voyeur of the writer's sensations." In this sense the lyric voice is both public and private, the solitary utterance drawing us in seductively the way a whisper spoken directly to us will, an author's voice that can bring the solace of comradery to a reader.

~ ~ ~

Usually, when I have trouble sleeping, I slip into the downstairs bed next to my study and, propped on pillows, reread "Earth's Body" from *Staying Put* by Scott Russell Sanders, the pages lit by a single lamp. The essay describes a night when Sanders can't sleep because he fears death. "Surely you know the place I'm talking about," he writes speaking to me as he traces the grain in his oak table with his finger. "You have skidded down the slope to oblivion, for shorter or longer stays." Oh yes, he is speaking directly to me. "Nothing else in my life," he says, "not the tang of blackberries or the perfume of lilacs, not even the smack of love" he adds, glancing up at me from the page, "is so utterly fresh, so utterly convincing, as this fear of annihilation." He is a little embarrassed. *We* are a little embarrassed. "Such alarm over the quenching of mind's wavery flame! Is this any way for a grown man to feel?" But he speaks for both of us, and I nod in assent when he writes: "Suitable or not, it is what I do feel."

The identification of self and author in lyrical passages like this is the most intense source of intimacy in personal prose allowing writer and reader to probe mysteries together. I am not a passive listener as I read, nor is he simply talking to the darkness—he has me or someone like me in mind in his solitude, some "surely you" from the phrase "surely you know the place I'm talking about" who is of course all of us, and he has in mind a task or ordeal for us to undertake together. Later, after looking at his face glowing harshly in the mirror, rubbing the nubs of nighttime whiskers, noticing his head looks more like a skull each passing day—all experiences

I have had—and after itemizing other ways that his body is as worn down with the same bags and sags and slumps as mine, he does what I am not going to do though by now I would follow him anywhere. He takes our insomniac question—"If there is no room for hope in the cramped house of skin, and no security in the glimmerings of the mind, then what abides?"—and walks outside with it into the night.

I go with him on the page in his attempt to turn our insomnia into "living midnight," a phrase he will lead me to eventually, but first because he is a superb writer, he immerses me in the experience of walking in the dark, of pushing "against the darkness as against the black weight of water," by appealing to senses other than sight. Eyes alone won't give him the answers that we need. "The air sizzles with insect song. Crickets and grasshoppers warn and woo, rubbing their musical legs." He compares them to the rattle sounds of beans in a pan, the bangles of dancers, and waves withdrawing from stones. There is romance in the air, he insinuates, though not the human kind. "Dozens of species combine to make this amorous hullabaloo." And, since he is an accomplished guide, and has me in mind, he gives a hint of where all this is going: "I let myself walk out onto the lawn trusting that the earth will uphold me even though I cannot feel the ground."

We spend a lot of time out there together, though I remain snugly in my downstairs bed. He remembers passages from the Bible and poets like Walt Whitman and Robert Browning, most of which I am familiar with because, well, I'm a reader too. *His* reader. Later he has a memory of his grandmother and thinks of his wife and children in bed. "While my mind rushes hither and yon," he writes in this book, called *Staying Put*, "my body stays put." The butterfly and the diving bell again. But in the midst of this swirl of thoughts and memories he does something I would never seriously do, really, although I have done it maybe as a joke. He walks up to one of the two large maples in his yard and, standing on the thick and twisted roots, wraps both arms around the trunk pressing his cheek into the bark, and even though I cannot quite picture myself doing that I feel the rumple under my toes and the woody crust against my face. "Earth is sexy," he proclaims, "just as sex is earthy," and "body and land are one flesh."

What do we hope for when we open a book like this in the middle of our night of fears? "Eternal life, I suppose" is Sanders' answer, though he is quick to add that the eternal life he is talking about "is not some aftertime, some other place, but awareness of eternity in this moment and this place." He begins with the earth and his own body which "by casting shadows, seem to be the opposite of light." Then, in this essay that is essentially one, long lyrical passage written just for me but with everyone in mind, he writes this:

> But if you have gazed up through the leaves of a tree at the sky, if you have watched the jeweled crests of waves, or held a shimmering fish in your hand, or lifted your palm against the sun and seen ruby light blazing through the flesh of your squeezed fingers, you know that matter is filled with fire. Matter is fire, in slow motion. Einstein taught us as much...The resistant stuff we touch and walk on and eat, the resistant stuff we are, blood and bone, is not the opposite of light but light's incarnation.

It is an epiphany of course, a flash of insight into one of life's mysteries. The science helps, the discovery that all matter is energy, "fire in slow motion," proving that the blood and bones of our bodies are "not the opposite of light but light's incarnation," but the examples of translucence cinch the deal with me. The light through leaves, the glitter along waves, the fish "shimmering" in his hands which are my hands when I was a boy, and above all the fingers pressed together and glowing in sunlight—all of these images make the ephemeral real, and although I have read this essay on many nights and I am not outside with him except in words, I hold my hand up to the lamp and watch the ruby glow pass through the clamped edges of my fingers.

Yes, I am light too!

It is here that he introduces the phrase "living midnight" which he found in *The Secret of the Golden Flower*, a Taoist book of wisdom. Living midnight is the ordeal of passing through the still hour of our worst fears of annihilation. On the other side of it is the answer to the question that he and I took into the sleepless dark, the one about what abides when this "cramped house of skin" dies. It is eternal light incarnated for now as you and me. By enduring this midnight of the soul, you can come out on the other side renewed, not beaten, to accept the "private extinction" of your own death and "return to daylight charged with passion and purpose." He lives through it by hugging a tree. I live through it by hearing his words in my head. What brings comfort are not the events in the essay, but the intimacy of our shared longing and the artistry of its lyric voice in shaping those longings. It is "an utterance for us to utter as ours," not his or mine alone, but "ours." Eked out by all writers one letter at a time and spoken for you, yes "surely, you," it has the power to transform sleepless hours into living midnight.

Ya Mismo

> Better to stop
> just shy of the brim
> than
> slosh over.
> —Lao Tsu

I have a sudden and vivid premonition of my basement flooding. Before leaving home, I had filled the reservoir of our homemade waterfall with a hose from our house, and, as I weave my way through Atlanta traffic, I wonder if I thought to undo the nozzle from the spigot. My wife and I are heading toward the airport for a Christmas-time trip to Ecuador to visit our daughter, Alice. While we are gone the temperatures are expected to sink into the teens at home, and if the hose is still connected to the house, water trapped in the pipes will freeze.

As I drive, I see in my mind ice choking the stem, cracking the seal around the valve seat, and splitting the tubing that runs into the house. While pulling into the HOV lane, I watch in a mental time-lapse trance as the ice in the faucet and pipes thaws and water leaks from the split in the pipe above my workbench, a mere trickle at first, but soon a gusher, pouring into the house with no one to stop it. I watch the water meter spinning, the basement filling like a swimming pool.

I can't tell Barbara. She is busy enough keeping an eye on my driving. It would only worry her and ruin the trip, so I cast a quick smile her way, as I follow the traffic down I-75 past Georgia Tech and MLK Drive, but in my mind I see the pockets of the pool table in our basement filling with water, the TV popping once, its great, blind eye filling with tears, books lifted in rows off of the shelves as they ride the rising tide, and, saddest of all, my guitar floating in its case toward the top of the stairs like a casket born on shifting shoulders.

~ ~ ~

In Ecuador, Alice's bathroom doesn't have warm water or a mirror, so I shave by feel. I touch the hairline at my right temple and begin there, running cold metal across my skin. The only sound is the scraping as the blade follows the contours of my cheek and the gurgle as cold water swirls down the drain. I try to keep water out of my mouth—the tap water in Ecuador makes Americans sick and even the Ecuadorians don't drink it— but I know I am becoming a little paranoid. I'm just *shaving*, I admonish myself. Still the thought crosses my mind, and I keep my lips shut tightly. Before I leave the bathroom, I wipe down the floor tiles with a towel. Some slow leak keeps Alice's floor a little wet, and I worry about us slipping. Naturally, I think about the basement at home too and have to shake my head to keep the gloomy premonition away.

Nothing I can do about that now.

There are other inconveniences in my daughter's apartment in the small town of Bucay. Roosters are everywhere and they must be blind because they crow at all hours of the night. During the dry season, the electricity goes off for several hours each day without warning. There is no hot water and in the wet season, Alice tells me, the cold water also goes off inexplicably for several hours each day. And even when the water is on it can be tricky. Before I shower I have to walk behind the apartment to the tiled tubs and basins that make up the open-air laundry area and arrange spigots and cut-off valves so that water will flow into Alice's bathroom, but no sooner do I finish my shower than the water goes off again. I crack the back door ajar holding a towel at my waist to see a neighbor rerouting the pipes so that his daughters can do the wash. As I dress, the lines strung above the patio fill with brightly colored clothes as the girls chatter and laugh. Alice would have to wait a while to take her shower.

How much of us remains when we travel 2,500 miles from home, I wonder as I sit on the end of my bed and eat a pastry I would not normally allow myself? When we set the self on the tray of some far-off place, what sloshes over the rim?

I hear Alice stirring.

"You don't have a mirror," I say when she traipses past me groggily.

"I don't need one." She yawns, intent on getting to the bathroom. "I'm always beautiful."

She stops and turns toward me, head tilted, eyes a little puffy, hair flopping in rich, dark waves about the neck and shoulder of her t-shirt.

"That's what I tell myself, anyway."

Alice is a Peace Corps volunteer in her first year of service, and she has just moved into this apartment, so she does not yet know the significance of the girls gossiping and giggling outside as they do laundry or the unfortunate implications of the brightly-colored clothes hanging above the veranda behind her place. She steps on the soggy mat in the bathroom and pushes it aside with her bare foot as she closes the door. I hear her turn the squeaky shower knob and groan.

~ ~ ~

I have trouble keeping the flooded basement out of my mind, and on the long bus ride into the Ecuadorian hills with Barbara and Alice, I find myself trying to picture the scene at home just before we left. Did I disconnect the hose? If so, all is well. Barbara and I had debated about whether to leave the waterfall on while we were away or drain it. Usually we leave it on all of the time, but we were worried that winter ice might cause it to freeze this time. In the end we agreed that it would be safer to let it run since the full basin would be less likely to crack and running water reduces the chances of the whole unit freezing. But I did drain it to clean out the basin as a precaution, and I remember positioning the end nozzle of the hose under a stone at the lip of the basin and walking back to turn on the water at the house.

Even now as the bus negotiates the twists and turns up the Ecuadorian Andes, I can close my eyes and see the waterfall as I refilled it. Water felt its way over rocks, the stream spilling in a small bell shape where several liquid braids came together. Here and there where the water hit a jagged crag, it sent a spray into the air before it tumbled in a glassy tube into a basin filled with dark and twisted leaves. All the while, along a plastic tarp behind the stones, a shadow stream wound like a slick, black, undulating snake mimicking in solemn fashion the glitter above. Life abundant and the hidden life. Over and over the same water spun through the cycle, the twin streams always different, always the same.

When the reservoir was filled, I remember lifting the nozzle and walking back to the house, looping the end of the hose as I went. Riding the bus toward the mountain town of San Bartolomé, I picture the scene vividly having played it over in my mind several times daily since we arrived in Ecuador and can see it all until I come to the part about disconnecting the hose from the house. The memory rises to that brim and, just before lifting me over it, stops. A blank. I open my eyes as the bus enters a cloud forest above the fog line, the blurry scene outside our windows turning gray. Banana and plantain trees rise as undefined spectral forms above shadowy huts and houses. "Silhouettes of unlife," I write in my notebook. "Waiting life. The visible drifting away. All depth removed, all color, shape. All rendered the same."

"A floating world."

I could not remember disconnecting the hose for a reason, of course, a reason that had compelled me to turn off my computer that morning and walk into my yard looking for something, anything, to do. It was an e-mail that I had spent the morning writing but hesitated to send. When I try to remember what happened after I rolled up the hose, all I can see is my finger, aglow with the light from the monitor, hovering over the key that would send the e-mail on its way.

Fog outside the bus window gets thicker. I peer into a floating world of wide, folded banana leaves in silhouette and see a forest of guitar cases floating toward me in the mist.

~ ~ ~

San Bartolomé is a lovely cathedral town along the spine of Ecuador's Andean range. The cathedral itself rises in a three-story, white structure with gold trim and a bell tower topped with a gilded cupola. A two-story wing extends off to one side, probably a school since a playground is nearby and children walk everywhere in clusters of three and four wearing identical white and black uniforms some lugging book bags strapped to their shoulders. On the day we arrive, the white building stands out against the gray clouds piled along the darkened ridge line and looks more like a fortress than a church.

We had ridden up the mountain from the city of Cuenca to buy Alice a guitar from Juan Uyaguari, a master builder who has a shop nearby. Barbara, Alice, and I get off of the bus planning to walk about in the town, but we are nearly 9,000 feet above sea level, and the air is so thin that we have trouble catching our breath. We ask directions and make our way along a paved road to a cinderblock building with a large yellow guitar painted on a sign that reads "Guitarra." Inside we meet one of the apprentices who explains that they are out of guitars. They sold them all at a recent festival to vendors from Cuenca. He shows us a few damaged instruments and toy guitars and says that our best bet is to head back down the mountain and check the shops in the city.

Disappointed, we walk back to the bus stop in the center of town, our steps measured and slow as if we are wading into thick water, our breathing labored. At the center of town Alice buys an ice cream on a stick at a small general store and asks the proprietress when a bus would be coming through.

"A qué hora sale el autobús?"

"El autobús?" the lady says with a shrug when she hands Alice her change, looking over the counter at the road as if the bus might already be there.

"Ya mismo," she answers and smiles wanly.

"It's a hard phrase to translate," Alice explains as we walk to the spot indicated by the lady at the store where Barbara was waiting for us. "Literally it means 'already the same,' which makes no sense," Alice says with a laugh, "but in Ecuador it means that the bus could be coming right now or in a few hours or next week. Or it could take forever." She shakes her head, licking the ice cream. "It's irritating, but it comes in handy, and I've started using it."

I look down the road. No sign of the bus.

"At my wedding, I'm going to say it with my vows," she adds wryly, hand over heart, intoning the words: "To love and cherish *ya mismo*.'"

She laughs again, an explosive quick laugh that causes the corners of her eyes to crinkle.

Now or forever, I think.

Already the same.

~ ~ ~

We found the guitar at La Bahia in downtown Cuenca. We checked several shops and this one had the best selection of Uyaguari guitars. I have been playing guitar since I was a boy and knew what to look for. I let Alice choose the ones that she liked, and then I brought them to pitch and played. I let her listen—they all had a deep, resonant tone—and I felt the action. I also checked to see if the neck was true by sounding a harmonic, touching the string lightly at the twelfth fret and comparing it to the actual note sounded there. We eventually settled on one with a lovely sunburst body and mahogany top that played easily.

When I play the guitar, time stops, and no matter where I am, I feel at home. It is not the sound really that causes me to relax, though I have always loved the tone of the guitar and often lose myself in it. "Sometimes I just play a chord and listen," I tell Alice. "You don't need to be able to play songs right away." The sound causes me to forget where I am, releasing me to an everywhere, and I can stay there a long time. But it is the feel of the guitar that grounds me and makes that everywhere a home. The body resonates through my torso as I cradle the instrument in my lap, like a lover, I used to think, but now, as I get older, it feels more like a child. And I sing to it, of course. Was it Beethoven who felt the resonance of his music in his piano after he could no longer hear? Something like that happens to me when I play the guitar, and I am filled with a sense of belonging.

Several nights later we show the guitar to one of Alice's fellow Peace Corps volunteers who lives in Cumanda, a neighboring town. Amanda is tall and blonde and athletic, a star on the local basketball team, and she is adored by men here. She tells the story of people warning her of the dangers of rumors when she accepted a ride home from a married man. Several *different* people, she said sarcastically. "It was just a three-mile ride home in the middle of the day!"

Amanda and my daughter don't have much in common. Amanda is from Portland, nearly a continent away from Alice's home near Atlanta, and Alice prefers a quilter's hoop to a basketball, but the two of them share English and the challenge of learning a new language, and often get together to eat and talk. Tonight, after a chicken dinner, Barbara, Alice, Amanda, and I sing Christmas songs while I play the new guitar.

Barbara knows all the verses, and the rest of us can join in on the choruses, so we sing on into the night. I wonder what the neighbors think. They certainly know our versions of the songs. In the bus station at Guayaquil, I watched a waif-like Ecuadorian girl in shorts and a t-shirt, rocking back and forth on her heels singing "Here We Go A-Caroling" in English. Enormous speakers under a decorated evergreen blared out other Christmas carols from home: "Santa Claus is Coming to Town," "I Saw Mommy Kissing Santa Claus," and, of course, "White Christmas," with Bing Crosby giving his iconic, mid-western, ba-ba-ba-boo lilt to the lyrics. I doubt, though, that Alice's neighbors have heard ordinary Americans singing the songs with more love than talent.

"This is hard," Amanda says after we have been going on for about an hour, fighting off nostalgia, but immediately she suggests "I Saw Three Ships" followed by "Oh Little Town of Bethlehem" and "Away in the Manger." She has been in Ecuador for a year and has not been back to Portland, afraid that if she goes home, she won't come back, though she is due to meet her folks in Miami after Christmas, a compromise. "If I saw the farms and the land, it would be hard to leave," she says, her skin glistening from the December heat in Bucay.

When I ask Alice what she has learned about herself in the Peace Corps, I am surprised by her answer. "I get frustrated easily here," she says. "I know that about myself. I get tired, not just with Ecuadorian friends but with English speakers." Of all of our children, Alice has been the most social with a cadre of close friends stretching back to grade school, and she keeps up with them all, but here, in a foreign country, she prizes solitude.

"Do you need time to be alone?"

"Yes, I guess that's it."

She tells the story of her host family confronting her *en masse* one afternoon afraid that something was wrong with her because she wanted time by herself. She assured them that she was fine. "Talk to me first," she said, "before you hold another family gathering."

"The Peace Corps is a great place for checking in on the self," Amanda explains as we walk her back to Cumanda along a dark road that crosses a dilapidated train trestle. It is late and we insisted that she not walk home alone. "I'm young and malleable and it's good to learn about myself. I'm not a patient person, but I know now that a project will get done in its own time."

"Ya mismo?" I ask, and we laugh.

We pick our way carefully around the broken crossties holding our arms out slightly for balance, like children.

"The Peace Corps is a great life check."

~ ~ ~

It took me nearly two weeks to write the resignation letter, the one that was on my mind as I gazed at the waterfall in my backyard, an e-mail I had planned in my head for months. I was not retiring entirely because I will still keep my classroom job for a while, but I was relinquishing my administrative responsibilities, a first step toward a complete retirement in a few semesters from a lifetime of teaching. Serving in this position had "been the highlight of my professional career," I wrote in the e-mailed letter. "It has brought me both joy and a sense of accomplishment." After composing the letter, and filing it away, revising it, and filing it away in daily succession, I sat at last at the keyboard, my finger poised over the key that would transmit the message to my superiors, and hesitated. I'm not young, and I doubt that I'm malleable, but it did feel like a life check.

I pressed "Enter" and the email flew off with a whoosh.

Where does it end, this letting go? I walked out in the yard past the garden spot and the bird feeder, scattering birds, and past the picnic table all beaten up and worn and gray with lichen. What happens when I come to the end of my list of chores? I looked at the lawn cart leaning against the house with the shovel propped against it. I turned and my gaze fell on the shaggy trunk of the Leland cypress I had planted years ago. Then I heard the waterfall. A reprieve! One more chore. I hooked up the hose and opened the nozzle, and as the basin filled, I watched, the lines of Lao Tsu floating in and out of my awareness. "Nothing on earth yields as cunningly as water." A little bored, I let my finger play along the spillway ledge and rearranged a few stones. "Better to stop just shy of the brim." Removing the nozzle, I walked back to the house already regretting that I had sent the letter when I remembered the last line of Lao Tzu's poem which I translate as "Work done? Retire, naturally."

~ ~ ~

Before we leave Ecuador we take a bus to downtown Cuenca to buy a Panama hat for me at Barranco's. The room has a slanted skylight that illuminates a spacious room with a flotilla of hats that appear to wash toward us as we walk in the door. Women's hats with domed tops and wide brims tipping on racks, their fancy ribbons shimmering like bright snapping pennants. Men's hats on tables in piles listing to the left or right including very smart fedoras with a pinch in the crown and decorative bows in the band. Hats in garish colors float on air, thrown along the pegs of the sunny wall glowing red, yellow, green, chocolate, beige, and purple, and on the other wall, cast in shadows, the unblocked versions of hats drifting in stacks that spill onto one another in waves.

A surge of hats.

A tsunami of hats.

161

I want a straw fedora with a wide cleft, a slight pinch, a thin brim, and a chocolate-colored band. Barbara and Alice watch as I try on several samples until I find one that fits and looks right. The salesman allows me to choose from several textures, and I select a fine weave, soft to the touch. When I hold the blank in one hand it flops over of its own weight like pizza dough, and the salesman scoops it up ceremoniously in two hands and carries it to women for shaping and finishing off. He tells us that we can have some coffee while we wait. The whole process would take about twenty minutes.

"*Ya mismo,*" I think.

The phrase *is* handy, maybe too handy.

The coffee shop is upstairs, and to get there we have to go through an outdoor walkway that overlooks Cuenca. A colorful map of the city made from local tiles stands on display and above that Cuenca itself, buses rumbling down wide avenues of the new suburb giving way, as the eye looks up, to taxis and cars snaking into the twisting alleys of the old city. We buy our coffees and cokes and sit in a room sectioned off by large pillars filled with artistic graffiti in pen and ink. Travelers around the world have written messages there in fancy script and many of the drawings are accomplished. One shows the face of a lovely young woman in repose, hair dark with glistening highlights and black eyes set wide beneath long lashes and thin eyebrows. In her hair she wears a flower, and she holds her shoulder up against her chin as if she has just awakened. Her mouth is a red pout or pucker, it is hard to tell which, and the blue-black hair flows down her back and under her cheek, dark curls scalloped along the wave poking up here and there and twisting over the wrist of her hand which rests just below her face. Seductive—that's the word that comes to mind when I look at the image. Above her in bold script someone has written a line of poetry signed with the name Bernardo Arguello: "La vida es maravillosa! Y no se repite."

When we return to the shop, the hat is ready. It feels almost weightless when I hold it in my hand, the straw silky to the touch. The weave begins in the center of the top, so when I look at it from above it makes a series of small, woven concentric circles at the crown, but when I tilt the hat to the side, I see circles ride up the fedora shape, the weave rising in a wave of stitches before disappearing in the tuck of the band. Like skin, like a cheek.

Life is wonderful!—without repeats.

We decide to ship the hat. Such a delicate thing would never survive the plane ride home. The clerk slides it into a sturdy box and looks up our postal zone on his computer.

"How long will it take?" Barbara asks.

Alice translates for her.

"Ten days, maybe two weeks," the clerk says in English.

Barbara pauses for a moment and laughs at herself.

"As if it matters," she says. "It's a *summer* hat, and it's probably snowing at home now."

~ ~ ~

The house did not flood. The first thing I did after parking the car in the driveway was check. The hose lay coiled where I had left it, the nozzle unattached to the faucet. Barbara laughed when I told her.

"You should have said something. I *saw* you undo it."

The guitar, I noticed when I walked downstairs, sat dry in its corner, and the pockets on the pool table had not filled with water.

163

But it was cold. Ice in the waterfall had grown thick while we were away, the upper ledge flaked with icicles, like the eyebrow of a grizzled wizard. Thin layers of glaze had piled up over time creating smooth, opalescent formations that looked like sea creatures, the foam freezing into the shape of the flowing water, arriving and becoming simultaneously, though water hidden behind the ice was still moving.

Flowing ice. Icy flow.

I reached out to touch the nub of a frozen dolphin caught mid-leap. *La vida es maravillosa!* Life abundant and the hidden life.

Y no se repite.

I have been and will be already the same.

~ ~ ~

According to the *Tao Te Ching* the ancient masters, who could fathom the unfathomable, were "wary" by nature, like old men "tiptoeing across a frozen stream in winter." The danger made them alert and watchful because the profound came on them before they knew it, "like ice when it begins to thaw."

A week or so after we got home, a package arrived from Ecuador, a brown box dented and nicked from traveling across two continents. It said "barranco, hechos a mano, naturalmente clásicos." I waited until I got home to open it, worried that the hand-made and naturally classic contents had been damaged, but when I lifted the hat and held it out for inspection it was perfect. The box had taken all of the blows and the Panama emerged unscathed. I ran my hand along the crown, my fingers flowing over the contours of pinch and brim like water.

THE BOOK OF KNOWLEDGE

In 1952, when I was three, my parents bought a set of *The Book of Knowledge,* ten hefty volumes bound in maroon leather, each filled with questions from "The Department of Wonder." Like sentinels posted at the gates of wisdom, the books stood proudly on a shelf between the glossy forelocks of equestrian bookends, each volume embossed with a golden torch. It was, my mother explained in one of the hundreds of letters she wrote to my grandmother, a purchase as much for her as for her boy: "I have really been enjoying it. I've been studying the subjects of music and art so far." Reading in *The Book of Knowledge* was one of the ways she fended off the depression that swept over her during these years, especially when my father traveled. "That is how I've been spending some of my evening while Max is away."

The Book of Knowledge evolved from *The Children's Encyclopædia,* the inspiration of Arthur Mee, born to a working-class family in Stapleford, England, whose formal education ended when he was fourteen. Questions posed by Mee's daughter, Marjorie, were the direct inspiration. In his letter "To Boys and Girls Everywhere," published in the first volume of *The Children's Encyclopædia,* Mee writes that Marjorie's mind was filled with "the great wonder of the Earth. What does the world mean? And why am I here? Where are all the people who have been and gone? Where does the rose come from? Who holds the stars up? What is it that seems to talk to me when the world is dark and still?" Mee's wife had "thought and thought" about these questions "and answered this and answered that until she could answer no more. Oh, for a book that will answer all the questions!" she complained. *The Children's Encyclopædia* was born.

What set his book apart, Mee explained, was the belief in children's eagerness for knowledge and their capacity for wonder. But he knew that his book also filled an important gap for adults. It "had the power to make plain to the average man, woman, and child the aspects and imports of the problems which the very men who had wrested them from nature could not make so plain." It offered up the mysteries of the few for the rest of us. By the time *The Children's Encyclopædia* had evolved into *The Book of Knowledge*, Mee had added the "Department of Wonder," and each volume contained sections devoted to "wonder questions" like the ones Marjorie posed to her perplexed parents.

For my mother, who had dropped out of nursing school when she was nineteen to marry my father, the gaps in her education were becoming an embarrassment. Born Roberta Maxine Reinhardt and called Bobbie, she had been the darling of her parents and of the small Kansas town of Glen Elder where she grew up. Pretty and bright, she made nearly perfect grades but not without help. "As I remember I used to make A on every theme you wrote for me," she mentioned in one letter to my grandmother. A little unsure of herself when she entered nursing school in 1946, she created elaborate study schedules, but soon found that she was good at school and liked her classes, which included American literature as well as courses in child guidance, microbiology, the history of nursing, nursing arts, physical education, home economics, and something called "the Home Project." As she pursued her studies, she became more confident: "I'm so thrilled about my subjects. There is an awfully lot of reading to do, but it is interesting." Anxieties about how hard the classes would be proved unfounded and she flourished in the program. "I've been wondering how I would like my nursing subjects—it is play to study them."

After marrying, that confidence in her abilities slowly eroded, especially when my father joined the pharmaceutical company, American Cyanamid, as a managing director and our young family moved from Dodge City, Kansas, to Nanuet, New York, a suburb of the city. In the 1952 letter about buying *The Book of Knowledge,* she describes a lavish dinner party served by maids. "Of course, the conversation got around to operas and plays," she complains, "as it always does here"; she did not feel comfortable again, she adds wryly, "until they all started talking about the pigs in Missouri." She admits that it was "an educational evening" and, after it was over, "a nice experience to have" but laments that she was caught off guard: "had I known beforehand I would have studied up." *The Book of Knowledge* was her way to 'study up.' "I've done very little brain work since I got out of school," she admits. "All you have to do is move around and meet new people to realize how dumb you really are." For my mother the gilded volumes of *The Book of Knowledge* served as a self-help textbook on culture.

For me they were simply wondrous. I liked to lie on my stomach on the floor in front of the bookcase, my feet kicked up behind me, just taking in the strange and glorious pictures: color illustrations in soft pastels from *The Book of the Dead,* which was left, the caption inaccurately tells us, "in the tombs of Egypt for the dead to read." A black-and-white cartoon of the globe in a ball cap, beaded in sweat and pulling down on a scale, to illustrate "Volume, Mass, and Weight." A four-page spread called "The Glory of the Grass" with detailed colored drawings of foxtail, rye, oat, timothy, manna, bearded darnel, broom, barley, reed, and wheat. Another four-page spread of "Beautiful Birds of the World," with a peacock in full array on the first page, surrounded by a Blue Crowned Motmot, a Leadbeater's Cockatoo, and a Groove Pygmy Goose, along with nine other brightly colored birds. And in Volume Eighteen, the fourteen-page spread of butterflies and moths and beetles that begins with a Peacock Eye, an American species of butterfly, and concludes, 236 individual illuminated drawings later, with the European beetle called the Great Agrilus.

The famous frontispiece to the first edition of *The Children's Encyclopædia* shows a boy in knickers and girl in bloomers looking into a universe: a system of eight planets, alongside comets, stars, and galaxies, surrounding the sun, which sends a halo of sunbeams out into the darkness. But the inside cover illustration of each volume of *The Book of Knowledge* that I grew up with suggests a similar grandeur with a modern twist. In it, a boy in shorts and girl wearing a skirt stand alert and excited on a red book floating toward an island of worldly wonders, including a telescope, a pagoda, totem poles, a factory, the faces of Mount Rushmore, and a giraffe. Overhead soar a rocket, a dual-propeller commercial airliner, a helicopter, and some sort of futuristic V-shaped spacecraft. "Here is a gift to the nation," Arthur Mee wrote to the readers of *The Book of Knowledge*. "It is a story that will never fail for children who will never tire; and it is the best of all stories, told in the simplest words, to the greatest of all ends."

~ ~ ~

And what is the end? On April 6, 1961, when I was eleven, my mother drove into a park near Deerfield, Illinois, where we lived at the time, and killed herself with a gun. Whatever knowledge she had gleaned from those books, as well as all that was left in her heart and mind of love, joy, sorrow, and agony, was swept away too. The obliteration ripples out from there. My father did not talk about the past, and the subject of my mother rarely came up after my father remarried and the family began anew. I remembered almost nothing of my life or her life before the suicide except a few vivid flashes, images, really, with the rest blown away by her death, and for years I was resigned to my ignorance and, perhaps, even content with it. I grew up, raised by a caring stepmother who probably got more than she bargained for when she took on, along with my dad, my brother and me, and I acquired a wonderful older stepsister who socialized me, and we did not dwell on our history. I went to college and married, and when I was in my thirties, my grandmother gave me the letters of my mother, but by then I had a job and a family with four children. I worked hard and was not depressed or suicidal. Why would I want to read the letters of a mother who killed herself before I could even get to know her?

When I turned sixty, I was given a new office at work, and I used that change as an opportunity to discard files, magazines, and correspondence—the stuff that I had accumulated over the years. I gave away or recycled books that I thought I would never part with. My wife, Barbara, offered a rule of thumb: if you feel the urge to sneeze when you open it, toss it out. In the end I threw away or recycled fourteen large plastic bags of junk, and I drove back from the transfer station feeling lighter. But when I got to the boxes of my mother's letters, I could not throw them away. I held them in my hand—they were dusty and definitely gave me the urge to sneeze—but I could not shove them in a plastic trash bag.

I made a vow that if I kept them, I would read them.

~ ~ ~

So, at the age of sixty-one, I bought a set of the 1952 edition of *The Book of Knowledge,* like the ones that I'd had as a child, and I read my mother's letters. Barbara raised an eyebrow when I mentioned *The Book of Knowledge,* a twenty-volume set bound in ten thick books, since she had been trying for several years to weed old books from our shelves at home, just as I had at the office.

"Are you going to *buy* them?" she asked. I think she was making soup or maybe spaghetti.

"They have a set for $350 at Amazon."

Barbara, poker-faced, just kept stirring the pot.

Eventually I found a complete set available at AbeBooks online for $150 and put in my order. Sheepishly, I promised Barbara that I would keep the box they came in and resell them online as soon as I had finished with them.

When they arrived, they were as magnificent as I had remembered, each handsome volume feeling heavy in the hand. Substantial, I thought, cracking open the cover of Volume One. Quotations by the likes of Louis Bromfield, Eleanor Roosevelt, aviation pioneer Captain Harry F. Guggenheim, and Lou Little, the head football coach at Columbia University, added authority to weight.

"The poet Marlowe might have been thinking of *The Book of Knowledge* when he spoke of 'infinite riches in a little room,'" Mrs. James P. McGranery, a member of the National Executive Committee of the Girl Scouts of the USA, explained.

"There is only one good. That is knowledge," John S. Knight, the publisher of Knight Newspapers, announced, quoting Socrates while glowering at me from his photograph. He added a stern admonition:

"There is only one evil. That is ignorance."

We fanned the books out on the floor and began leafing through them, stopping at the colored spreads, Barbara running her fingers over the brightly illuminated pages. The books spoke of a time after the Second World War when knowledge and progress and hope were allies, a time that she and I remembered dimly now as we ended the first decade of the twenty-first century. Barbara found a page that asked, "Could We Ever Travel to the Moon?" and I cringed at the outdated question, but she smiled. "Listen to this," she said later, reading at random an article in Volume Thirteen called "Government and Taxes," which argued that simply taxing in proportion to income, as the Constitution says, is unfair. "Taxes should be levied in such a way as to establish equality of sacrifice between rich and poor."

"Equality of sacrifice," she repeated, "imagine that."

Before long she was eyeing the bookshelves we had been hoping to clear. "We'll make space right there."

"These books are pretty out of date," I said apologetically, opening a volume and resisting the urge to sneeze.

She was thinking about our new grandchildren.

"They could stand to read this."

She rapped the book with her knuckle. Decision made.

~   ~   ~

In retrospect I regret that I waited so long to read my mother's letters. There were 406 in all, carefully arranged by my grandmother in shoeboxes. Over time, as the family leafed through them, they had gotten out of order and had been placed in different areas of the house before most were carted off to the office. It was not until six months after I finally brought them home that I spread them out on a pool table and put them in order. I boxed them and marked off each of the years with strips of manila cardboard, tickets to the past extending back in time from 1960 to 1945, and one chilly morning in November 2010, some fifty years after my mother's death, I started to read the entire set through.

My mother's writing style is direct and friendly, and—since she saw my grandmother as a confidante, especially in the early years of her marriage—often candid. As she got older, and more troubled, she tried to hide her depression, but she had become so used to confiding in her mother that the truth comes out anyway. As I read about her life, my memories, lying like ashes in me, were sparked. The steady chronology of a letter or two each week allowed me to place the few vivid memories I had left in a context so that I saw how they fit and understood why they, of all in my lost past, had remained as a glowing remnant. My dad, in that time before I remembered him, came back clearly as well. Most of all, I got to know my mother at last, not the stereotypical fifties mother forced to play an uncomfortable role, though she was that, but the real person with her achievements and flaws and hopes and many, many fears. As she married, left college, moved away from home, and had children of her own, I watched her change and grow, darken and retreat. The return addresses evolved from "Bobbie Reinhardt," a young nursing student in 1942 at the University of Kansas Hospital in Kansas City, to "Mrs. M. J. Harvey" in Dodge City in 1947. By the time the family had moved to New York, she dropped the "Mrs." altogether, and in Chicago in 1959 she retreated entirely by writing the return address using my father's name and title: "Dr. M. J. Harvey."

Every letter stood alone, capturing a particular time and, more important, mood, and yet each danced in consort with the others. As my mother married and had children, the mobile of her life grew heavier and more complicated, with many moving parts, and by the time of her death the structure groaned under the weight of accumulated anxieties and regrets. Armed with letters and a children's encyclopedia, I was determined to know who this woman was, and, with luck, claim a legacy of beauty and wonder from a devastating event.

~ ~ ~

Wonder Question: "Does the earth make a sound as it rotates?"

"No," *The Book of Knowledge* answers, the "earth spins silently in space. It spins all in one piece, and that means not only the solid earth and the waters but the blanket of air above us as well. All spins round, never pausing." Like some enormous Carny ride, the globe rotates at a thousand miles per hour, and yet the mobile over my shoulder hangs motionless by a thread and going nowhere, expectant and watchful as an acrobat holding a pose. "If the air stood still we might hear the earth whooshing through it," but the "air is part of the earth and moves with it," creating the illusion of stillness.

Even if we could step off of the earth like the boy and girl in the illustration for *The Children's Encyclopædia* and stand on some promontory separate from the planet and listen hard, we would not hear the earth spinning. The scene would unfold like a slow-motion silent film, the incredible rush of the whirling planet registering on our eyes like the imperceptible motion of the slow hand on a watch and on our ears as a held breath. The other celestial objects would lumber along in mute procession with vast stretches of nothing at all between them. To hear any sound, "we must have vibrations, or waves, or trembling." But space is a nearly empty vacuum, and no matter how dark and gloomy and terrifying emptiness may be, trembling requires "something substantial" to be felt.

In space there is "no substance to be set trembling."

~ ~ ~

When she was five or six, Roberta trembled beside a toy tricycle that was built to look like a single-prop airplane. My grandparents took a Brownie photograph of her standing beside the new toy, with the shingled side of their house as the background. The front of the trike had a propeller with a circle of pistons behind it, and the tailpiece at the end had numbers stamped in it to make it look authentic. The cockpit swooped down so that the rider could sit down completely and pedal. The toy is large, longer than she is tall, and it is clearly made of metal, with dimples where bolts attach the wheels to the body. The wheels are inflatable rubber tires with shiny metal hubcaps. In the photograph my mother poses proudly, wearing Mary Janes, stockings, a pleated dress, a V-neck sweater, a beaded necklace, and a knit cap. She is dressed for cold weather and, since she was born in June, this is probably not a birthday gift but a Christmas present. A shadow of some sort, perhaps the shadow of a tree, rises like a thin stream of smoke from behind her shoulder and spreads across the shingles of the wall, the adumbration folding ominously and turning on her like the black contrail of a plane in trouble. Hurtling through space at a thousand miles an hour, my mother may be trembling a bit from the cold, but otherwise she does not feel the future rushing toward her. She cannot see the crash ahead. The air, after all, is moving too, at one with a planet of rocks and stones and trees and spinning silently in a universe largely without substance. The girl who is my mother leans casually with her open hand on the wing of the toy while a ribbon of black smoke billows across the shingles behind her. Unaware and smiling, she looks directly at me.

~ ~ ~

Wonder Question: "Why do faces in some pictures seem to follow us?"

"The rule is very simple," *The Book of Knowledge* says. "If the sitter is looking at the painter or at the camera, then wherever you stand, he will seem to be looking at you." I lift the photo of my mother beside her new toy and tilt it under the lamp, first to the right and then the left, and her eyes stay on me even though the nose of the airplane seems to bob away and return, the world of the photo turning on the axis of her eyes. And her smile—yes, it also seems to keep smiling at me, no matter which way I turn the stiff and fading image.

But this rule, as stated here, is not as simple as *The Book of Knowledge* likes our wonders to be. There is the word "seem" in the phrase "he will seem to be looking at you," which is never simple. It drains the ink out of the words around it, appropriating them subjunctively. The little mood shift invites supposition into the mix, leaving the facts behind. It is the "seem" of what is not, the "seem" of absence that these pictures in the end make me feel, a magical "seem" bringing in its wake the black smoke of an apparent accident that has not happened yet in the photo, but has already happened a long time ago in life. Nothing is looking at me in this photograph, although it is smiling broadly into the camera and trembling slightly in the cold, a trembling I can't feel because of the nothing between us, and this nothing follows me no matter which way I turn it.

~ ~ ~

Thirty years later, in November 1960, my grandmother "got word" that my mother was in the hospital. I was eleven and we were living in Deerfield, Illinois. The phrase "got word," taken from notes that my grandmother wrote near the end of her life, is portentous. It means that my mother was in no condition to write to her or call her and that my father, whom my grandmother never trusted, had to break the news. If I grow still and close my eyes, I can imagine the sound of the conversation, him offering up the facts through the mixture of sympathy and complaint he used to calm anxious colleagues, and her, with her Kansas reticence, replying in tight-lipped, staccato phrases. I cannot even begin to imagine their words. She and my grandfather "left immediately by train for Deerfield." They stayed with my brother and me until my mother killed herself five months later.

My grandmother never talked to me about what happened when my mother was institutionalized for depression, but she did talk to Barbara, who wrote letters to her on a regular basis until my grandmother died in 1986, and who was probably my grandmother's dearest confidante at the end of her life. She told Barbara that when they released my mother from the hospital, the doctors said that they "had done everything that they could" and were still pessimistic. "When she left the hospital, your grandmother knew she would do it," Barbara said when I asked her about it again this morning. She had told me about the conversation before but to make her point clear now she put it this way: "when your mother left *that morning*" on the day she killed herself, "your grandmother knew she would do it."

After I graduated from college, I asked my father about my mother's suicide. We were riding in silence in his car early in the morning.

It was still dark outside, the only light the blue glow from his dashboard. I know he didn't want to talk about it, but he wanted to answer my questions. Nothing made her happy, he told me, and the doctors could do nothing for her. "They tried everything," he said, an echo of my grandmother's words. He said that she bought a .44 caliber gun, which is a large bore. "She *meant* to do it, to end things." So, she drove to the park and killed herself. It pained him to say this, I could tell. I do not want to underestimate the difficulty of living with someone who is clinically depressed. I know, now, from reading her letters that he tried to make her happy, and he was very good at making others feel happy, but in the long run he could not work that charm on her. He took a long drag from his cigarette, squinted, and stuffed the butt in his ashtray, slowly exhaling the smoke as the car hurtled down the highway, waiting for my next question, but I did not ask any more. We rode silently into a pre-dawn darkness illuminated by the blue light from the dash.

I turn to *The Book of Knowledge* for answers to questions I didn't ask.

~　~　~

In its 7,606 pages, *The Book of Knowledge* has no entry for suicide. It has no entry for insomnia, alcoholism, or addiction either. There is an entry for ragweed, but not for rage. In the age of anxiety there is no entry for anxiety. No entry for depression without 'Great' in front of it. The entry on sex is limited to plants and flowers. There is no entry for conformity or blandness or dullness or insipidity—and this was the 1950s! Sometimes I wonder about *The Book of Knowledge.* I find an entry for Peter Pan, of course, but none for Cyril Ritchard. No entry for either "Fever" *or* Peggy Lee. Nothing on the doldrums, the dumps, the mulligrubs, or the blues. No blue funk or the blahs. Nothing on grief—*grief!* No entry for funeral, burial, interment, last rites, cortège, mourners, pallbearers, or pall. No entry for self-murder, self-slaughter, self-destruction, and no entry for self. No entry for hara-kiri (which is a little surprising) or suttee (which is not). There are several entries under medicine, but no cure for despair, despondency, sadness, sorrow, unhappiness, melancholy, or gloom. Doom does not make the pages. Nor agony nor suffering nor woe. In *The Book of Knowledge*, no *woe!*

~ ~ ~

Wonder Question: "What is everything?"

In the late 1950s, after the doctors try everything else, they strap the patient to a gurney in a hospital room and tape the leads of a heart monitor to her chest. They do not inject her with an anesthetic for pain or use muscle relaxers to reduce the chance of bone fractures and other injuries when the arms, legs, and chest rise against the restraints, but they do place a block in her mouth so that she cannot bite her tongue while the procedure is performed. They attach electrodes on either side of her face at the temples after applying a conductive jelly so that an electrical current will pass into her head and brain more easily. Once she is ready, the doctor turns on a machine that sends a steady stream of electricity into her skull, the current running between the right and left lobe of her brain for twenty seconds, inducing a grand mal seizure and leaving her unconscious, usually for about a half hour. No one knows for sure what happens in her brain as her eyes roll back and her body stiffens. The shock of electricity may slow overly agitated mental activity or dull the brain receptors, altering mood. It may release neuropeptides that ease depression. Or it may cause brain damage. Electroshock therapy helps many people, but, as one critic put it, the procedure is "like playing Russian roulette with your brain."

What is everything in the late 1950s?

It is a very sad figure of speech come true.

~ ~ ~

When I was a boy, I lay in bed at night listening to my parents fight downstairs. The arguments began as conversation mixed with the clinking sound of ice in glasses, the words spoken softly, clipped and brittle, dipping to inaudibility when whispered. The clicking of tree branches that is prelude to the storm. Eventually the voices rose until the two were shouting and finally screaming furiously, the sound coming through the walls in unarticulated growls. I don't think they ever hit each other, but sometimes they broke glasses and ashtrays. Dad may have caught her arms when she took drunken, limp, and futile swings at him. I think I saw that once.

I was too afraid when they fought to move and lay wrapped under a cocoon of sheets and blankets that felt like safety but acted like an echo chamber, amplifying and distorting the low rumble until the roar, punctuated now and then with a slam or a crash, spilled over me in torrents. I waited, understanding nothing, absorbing it all. It was only when the yelling was done that the silence after the curses brought me out of bed to the top of the stairs to be sure that they were all right. I usually walked down a few steps and leaned forward, peering between the balusters in order to see into the kitchen, blinking at the fluorescent glare. One night, they caught me. I can picture the tableau even now. My dad, his sleeves rolled up, facing a wall, my mother sitting bent over in a kitchen chair with her back to him, crying in gasps, mascara running down her cheek.

"Oh, no," she says when she turns and sees me running back upstairs.

The next day my father pulled me aside and asked what I had heard.

"You were fighting," I said.

He corrected me. They were not having a fight, but a "discussion."

"That's what adults do," he said.

The memory of the fight followed by the conversation with my dad glows like a lit match in the darkness that is my past. Here is another lit match. From my bedroom I see a light in the hall, soft this time like the glow of a candle. Drawing the twisted sheets up around my shoulders, I hear the clank of the changer and the long wavering whoosh and whir when the needle hits the disc. Clink of ice in a glass. Swoosh of a magazine dropped to the floor. My mother turns up the volume, and soon Peggy Lee's voice fills the house to the corners, beating back gathered silence. I slip out of bed and hide at the top of the stairs to watch. Snapping fingers, slapped cymbal, thud of a double bass and drum, and a lone, plaintive female voice. Mom's there, her back to me, her face partially visible, lit by the glow of the console. She sways, drink in hand, and sings, watching the record spin, holding the notes out for no one, trying to sound good.

"What a lovely way to burn," she croons. "What a lovely way to burn."

~ ~ ~

The fights and my mother singing "Fever" happened before my grandparents moved in with us in November 1960. Peggy Lee's new song, "Fever," was the rage, and my parents had the album in their record collection, and this record followed my family long after my mother died. I remember it because of the distinctive cover photograph of Peggy Lee in a black cocktail dress, her pale skin and platinum-blonde hair set against a blue background. The album was released in May 1960. So, the fights and the drinking alone while singing into the stereo console must have happened between May of 1960 and November 1960, in the time just before my mother was hospitalized for depression.

During 1959 and 1960 my dad was gone most of the time on business trips and to take courses in business management in St. Louis. My mother thought he was pushing himself too hard. He had developed an ulcer and the doctor recommended that he cut back on his work. "Sometimes I think we are crazy," my mother wrote on June 24, 1959. "The men work at such a pace and under so much pressure." During that time, she must have confronted him about the burden that the maddening pace and heavy responsibilities of his job placed on him and the family: "We discussed this when he was sick and I suggested a change, but he said he liked his work and seems to have the ability so we decided it would be a matter of adjusting our leisure time to make it workable."

I know what those "discussions" sounded like.

In the end my dad had his way. The trips continued. "Max has been in St. Louis," she writes on March 26, 1959, and on July 9 she mentions that "Max has been to St. Louis since Tues. will be back tomorrow." These business trips to St. Louis run like a refrain after 1959 until the letters come to an abrupt halt in June 1960, within a month of the release of the album that contained "Fever." The memory of that song may be the last message I have from my mother since it probably came after the last letter.

My stepmother tells me that she met my father in St. Louis.

My mother seems unaware of infidelity during 1959 and early 1960. In the letters she appears to be genuinely concerned about the problems related to Dad's job. What upset her was the pressure that it put on their lives. It did damage to their friends, some of whom became alcoholics, made my father ill, and saddled my mother with social responsibilities she could not, given her tendency to depression, handle. I sense in all of the letters from that time a desire to live in a way that reduced the strain on everyone, and I suspect that the conversation about leaving the company was real. Dad's ulcer and her exhaustion only reinforced the idea that their loveless marriage had to do with the demands of his career, not another woman, but sometime in June of 1960 she must have figured out that Dad had found love elsewhere, and the letters stopped.

"Captain Smith loved Pocahontas," Peggy Lee sings in a verse that she wrote and added to her version of the song. They "had a very mad affair."

The depression that perched on my mother's life and led to her suicide on April 6, 1961, had many sources, but here is one black wing: On April 29, three weeks and two days after my mother's death, Dad married my stepmother.

"What a lovely way to burn," Peggy Lee growls four times at the end of "Fever." "What a lovely way to burn." In the penultimate line her voice rises in desire on the first word—"What"—before it slides down "a lovely way" to the last note, "burn," dying like the flicker of a heartache.

And the final line? It is a scorched whisper, a beckoning, and a come-on. It is a raised eyebrow. "What a lovely way to burn."

~ ~ ~

Wonder Question: "Who holds up the stars?"

The stars only appear to be nailed into fixed positions in the dome of the night sky and no one really holds them up for us. According to *The Book of Knowledge*, "all the stars—in fact, everything in the universe, asteroids, stars, galaxies of stars—all are moving through space at unbelievable speeds of many miles a second." The "great force of gravitation" holds them in check. "Each bit of matter in the universe pulls upon every other particle of matter," and this mutual attraction can cause collisions. "If one body comes too close to another body, the lesser is drawn into the greater and destroyed." But when the velocity of the objects and the distance between them is right they move in consort. In the end this apparently accidental dance of forces is "responsible for the balance and state of equilibrium in the universe."

On the day of my mother's death, I stared into trembling stars nailed into the night sky of my own making in the hope of achieving some equilibrium. I liked spinning in our newly renovated downstairs den, holding a Jetfire balsa-wood plane that I kept in my hiding place under the stairs. I usually got the planes at the five-and-dime when I visited my grandparents in Glen Elder, but they must have brought the plane to me because this memory is in Illinois. I can still picture these planes that I assembled myself and studied for hours. The wings were stamped with red designs marking the ailerons and flaps and labeled on one side with the name of the company, "Guillow's," and on the other with the name of the plane, "Jetfire." The cockpit was embossed on the fuselage and inside a pilot with a red helmet leaned forward. Meant to ride breezes, the glider is light in my hand. It has a small piece of metal folded over the nose for protection when it crashes against the walls of the house or lands on the concrete driveway, but I'm not allowed to fly it indoors, so I hold it and spin, making airplane noises and getting dizzy. When I stop, the room seems to keep on spinning and I wobble a bit as if I have taken a blow. I'm almost twelve. Too old to be doing this sort of thing.

My mother died on the day that my father planned to leave the family for good. In retrospect I know that he intended to start a new life for himself in Kentucky without my mother or my brother and me. Was he anxious or exhilarated when he left the house that April morning, relieved or scared? Or some other emotion I cannot even imagine. If on that day my grandmother knew what my mother would do, he may have too, but I'm not sure because, unlike my shrewd grandmother, he was an optimist. After he left, my mother bought the gun, drove to a park, stepped out of her car, and pulled the trigger. My grandparents, who knew it would happen, were taking care of my brother and me. When Dad found out, he came back for us.

In memory I was alone downstairs in the newly renovated den, killing time with this spinning game, when my dad arrived and the house began to fill with neighbors and my parents' friends. I heard the ringing doorbell of each new arrival. The hushed greetings. The whispers. The shuffle of feet over carpet as adults overhead approached each other. I am pretty sure that no one had told me what had happened yet. In my memory Dad would do that when we were on the train going to Kentucky. But I knew *some*thing because I hid under the stairs in my favorite hideaway and sat there a long time before anyone noticed my absence. The points of the nails that had been used to secure the treads to the risers of the stairway protruded overhead. Like stars they glittered in the crawl space, and I looked into them as I listened to the groan in the floorboards. Suddenly it grew silent, and I heard my father call for me. At first his voice was a question, but then, freighted with all of the tension of that day, it became a barked command. Soon others joined in, their anxious voices a keening chorus on my name.

A shadow passed over the risers.

"Who holds the stars up?" Marjorie Mee asked her perplexed mother.

I covered my ears.

~   ~   ~

Last September, when Barbara and I visited my stepmother in Kentucky, we spent a Saturday morning looking through pictures. Nearly eighty, she pulled them out of boxes one at a time with her arthritic fingers, stopping occasionally to talk, and the subject came around to my mother.

"No, honey," she said, when I asked if my mother bought the gun before that day. I'm sitting across from her at the kitchen table. Barbara, who is standing, stops flipping through pictures, and listens. "She bought it that morning. She killed herself in the park. A policeman saw her and thought it unusual so he watched. She stepped out of the car and then."

My stepmother puts her finger to her temple and lifts her eyebrows.

"Bam."

I look away. A cat waits in a crouch under the bird feeder in her neighbor's yard. I want to hate my stepmother for doing that, for being so distant from these events that she turns them into a cartoon. I have trouble getting the image out of my mind, her lips puckering on the single syllable, her finger on the trigger and her thumb tripping like an imaginary hammer. Barbara looks at her, and then me, dismayed I can tell, but also willing to let the moment pass without comment, urging me, with her glance, to do the same. She turns back to the pictures that she is flipping through. These events happened long ago involving a woman my stepmother never met. I may be hearing hard truths about my mother, but she is talking about a stranger, in plain language which is her way, and what she really wants to describe is her own loneliness and desperation.

"Neither of us had anybody," she said, referring to the time when she and my father first met in a bar, explaining that her first husband was impossible to live with, too. "I had nobody. Your dad had nobody."

Nobody.

Silenced for a moment by that story, we return to the pictures. Many of them show my stepmother with my dad through the years, but I pause over one in particular. In it, the two of them are preparing dinner. They both are young, in their thirties. My dad, heavyset in a dark shirt and white warm-up pants, has turned, startled by the picture, and his face, picking up the full impact of the flash, wears a customary carefree and bold look. He's making a salad and is, no doubt, about to tell a joke. The flash explodes like a supernova on the sliding glass door behind him, turning the rest of the glass black.

It is the image of my stepmother that holds my attention, though. She stands in the wood-paneled room, looking young and very pretty in a striped sweater and tight slacks, her nose aquiline and her hair all dark curls. She leans toward my father from behind as if she has some secret to share, but the easy-going intimacy of the photograph keeps no secrets. He came to her in St. Louis for fun, happiness, love, and sex. He came to escape a home full of woe, some of it, no doubt, of his own making—some, but not all. He was leaving us for this, that was the secret, and when my mother figured it out, she gave my brother and me to him, to them, with a single gunshot.

~ ~ ~

Wonder Question: "What is the sound of everything happening at once?"

"When a gun goes off," *The Book of Knowledge* says, "the flash and the report of the gun occur in the same moment." If we stand at a distance, the flash appears first, as a silent flare in the darkness, and the muffled blow of the sound arrives later, in an echo of the flash. So, if you stand at a safe distance half a mile away when the gun is fired, "you will not hear the sound for nearly half a minute."

"And yet," *The Book of Knowledge* adds, because it is fond of "and yet." "If we are very near the gun, we see the flash and hear the noise at the same time." At that range, you miss nothing. If you hold the gun to your body, you feel everything happening at once, and it reverberates until the trembling stops somewhere at the edge of nothing.

Turning the self into a nothing is a moral conundrum too difficult for *The Book of Knowledge* to crack. A literal self-contradiction, the answer even eluded Jesus. The Catholic poet Dante may have planted the suicides with other violent sinners in a deep ring of hell and tormented the poor souls with winged harpies, but the golden rule is about doing unto others, not doing the self in, and on suicide Jesus is silent. It wasn't until the nineteenth century that Immanuel Kant explained the immorality of suicide with his "categorical imperative." When faced with a moral dilemma, Kant argued, you should act so that your action becomes universal law. When you lift a gun to your temple to pull the trigger, you must imagine that the hands of all of the people in the world are required by your version of the moral law to lift a gun to their temples too. No one escapes the bullet in this game of Russian roulette. "Do you like this vision of the world?" Kant asks.

I give it a try and see my mother in the hall of mirrors within her moral imagination, every hand in the world holding a .44 lifted at her command, and she pulls the . . . but, no, that is not right.

Suicide is about the survivors.

Suicide is two boys and their father hurtled into darkness at the speed of a locomotive. The boys, sitting on the plush pile seat of a railroad car headed away from their home in Deerfield, Illinois, will never see their mother again, rarely speak of her again, rarely think about her again. Their father—a big man, bulging out of his suit—sits down on his haunches in front of them. Facing into the darkness ahead, he has been through hell and has been given one more impossible task, but he is a man who believes in taking charge and wants to fix things even when he can't, so he will do his job. The boys are headed backward into the night, the lights outside the window floating away from them, and I don't know if they are afraid or in shock or just tired.

Who knows what the younger one remembers? He is eight years old and has penetrating blue eyes. The older one remembers his dad looking down but only for a moment and then, as he always did when he spoke to people, looking directly into his sons' eyes and saying the impossible. I remember him speaking, his voice a mesmerizing low rasp conveying confidentiality this time as well as command, and I remember him reaching out with his arms to kind of hem us in as he spoke, his large arms coming out of the sleeves of his suit a bit as he extended them. I remember, or I think I do, the maroon plush of the seats in the Pullman and the windows black as we rode into the open fields of Illinois at night.

But I have no idea what he said.

~ ~ ~

Someone took pictures at my mother's funeral. I found them in a wicker basket with other photos and memorabilia. Several show the graveside service conducted on the open prairie of Kansas, the land that my mother wrote of "going back to" in her memory while living in New York. The photographs are mixed in with a nearly identical set of pictures from my grandfather's funeral, which came three weeks after hers, including a particularly sad one of my mother's and grandfather's graves side by side, her blossoms windblown and slightly wilted beside his new batch of greenery and white.

But the hardest pictures for me show my mother's open casket surrounded by a shower of flowers, a mound of red and white carnations, daisies, and pink mums. The coffin is draped in a spray of red roses, and my mother's body lies in a bed of satin, the opening of the casket draped in a transparent mesh. The picture of her face is very small, but I can see that her hair is pulled back from her forehead in tight curls. She wears a suit with a silk scarf at the neck, exposing the base of her throat. I find a magnifying glass that I keep with my dictionary, and examine the picture up close. The cotton and plaster of Paris that the morticians used to reconstruct the face make her cheeks look puffy and the dermal wax and restorative cosmetics hide her wounds and bruises under a shiny pastiness betraying the illusion of life. There is something wrong with the mouth, which has been stretched wide into a smile after the mortician pulled together the scalp, and the eyebrows are heartbreaking, dark and perfectly arched like wings, as if, after all, death took her by surprise, and maybe— who knows?—it did.

My gaze settles at last on her eyes. Leaning forward into the lens to see more clearly, I tilt the picture this way and that for a better look, before slumping back into my chair.

Faces in photos don't follow us if their eyes are closed.

~ ~ ~

Until I read her letters, those closed eyes were my mother's story, an image that I carried until I became a sixty-year-old man. And yet—because there is always this "and yet"—there is more, much more, and it is in the letters, not the photographs.

"We took our first drive yesterday," my mother writes on Monday, November 20, 1950, from a brick bungalow in Monsey, New York, when she and Dad first moved away from Kansas to live in the Northeast. "The scenery around here is gorgeous. We took the Hudson River Drive on the way up." She explains that she is sending pictures, and I find the colored postcards in my wicker box, stiff and pretty colorized photographs of West Point and the river, but her words say more than the pictures. "The river is very large, calm, and beautiful," she writes. Having lived in the prairie all of her life, she is unaccustomed to seeing large bodies of water and is filled with wonder. "Saw the ships and were quite thrilled—first large ones I've ever seen. We took Bear Mountain Drive home. We were sorry we didn't get to see all of this because it got dark before we got home. It is completely dark by five here."

My mother weathered the mental cyclone of depression much of her adult life, but there are moments in the letters when she paints, in words, another self, whole and wonder-struck, and the whirlwind stops. These moments often happen outdoors, or while looking outdoors, and

190

record a joyous embrace of a wide and open sky that may have evoked feelings of the family farm in Kansas where she and my grandparents picnicked while she was growing up. They are sublime glimpses of grandeur, often bounded by darkness, the blackness that finally claimed her, creeping in at the edges, but they are also marked by a brilliance of light and an expansive vista that is exhilarating. The sights transported her, lifted her momentarily out of the troubles of life; they helped her to be her best self and re-engage with family.

In one letter she describes a flight back from Kansas in prose reminiscent of her descriptions of seeing the Hudson River for the first time. "Had such a smooth flight from K.C. to N.Y. Slept part of the way. The plane was very crowded when we boarded so I had to sit on the inside seat of the three[-seat] row which was fine except I couldn't see out too well but thought the view of K.C. and Chicago were gorgeous. Looked like a huge Christmas display." She explains that she arrived early at LaGuardia and took the time to freshen up before meeting us. "When I walked out I saw Max & boys—called to them. The boys were so surprised for a second—I squatted on my knees—Ronnie said, 'Mommy' and gave me a big hug. I hugged Steve with my other arm. He put his arms around my neck and said 'Hello, Mommy.'"

After my mother died, I forgot the sensation of her touch and the sound of her voice. I could not hug a shadow. I could not fill her silence with my words.

Who is suicide? She was suicide.

She became her death.

And the pictures, hundreds of curled shavings of the past in a basket, did not bring her back. Even when my mother gazed directly into the camera, I knew that she was looking into a future that was already over with shadows like gun smoke folded into the glossy black-and-white. I needed a voice speaking in her present, not one whispering to posterity, a voice animated by the desire to capture the present for someone alive. *That* is the voice I heard in the letters. When I read them, I got to know her—for the first time, really—know her and miss her. Miss *her*, not some made-up idea of her. The pain, which had been nothing more than a dull throb, changed in character, becoming softer, more diffuse, and ardent like heartache.

"They each held on to my hands," my mother wrote, describing our triumphal exit from the airport at LaGuardia. "They kept talking to me about how happy they were that I was home—and sorta beamed."

~ ~ ~

Wonder Question: "Could we ever travel to the moon?"

"We know everything we need to know for the planning of such a trip," *The Book of Knowledge* claimed optimistically in 1952. Its writers argue that the first real problem will be creating a rocket with enough thrust to allow a "space-ship" to reach "escape velocity," the speed required to lift the ship beyond the gravity of the earth and let it float, unimpeded, toward the moon. The formula for determining this velocity is too complicated for *The Book of Knowledge* to make clear, so it asks that we accept on faith that by means "of a computation belonging to the realm of higher mathematics" the velocity required for a rocket to rise into space and escape the gravitational pull of the spinning earth is "7 miles per second." Once a rocket can attain that speed the "earth's gravity is powerless" to pull it down and the rocket can drift into the vast emptiness of silent space, leaving the weight of its earthly burdens behind.

Five years later, the Soviets rocketed a satellite into orbit.

~ ~ ~

At midnight on the last day of January in 1957, my mother and father woke me to watch Sputnik 2 cross the dome of the sky, and I don't remember it happening at all. I do remember Sputnik 1. We were still living in our house on Caravella Lane in Nanuet, New York, and many from the neighborhood, including my mother and me, had lined up on the dead-end street in front of our houses to see the first satellite propelled into orbit, but the memory of the second satellite is gone.

It was an anxious time internationally, causing Americans, like my mother, to have mixed feelings about the space race. "It is a shame," she wrote, that "the great event of launching a satellite into space has to be overshadowed with the fear that the Russians are a great deal ahead of us scientifically." At the dawn of the nuclear age, she lamented that the Soviets had "perfected the intercontinental missile" and wondered about the ability of America to prevail. "It makes us all realize we have been complacent." Despite these anxieties, she wrote that we were all "very excited" and that Sputnik 1 was a "spectacular sight."

Sputnik 2 caused a stir because it carried Laika, the dog, but by this time our family had a new set of anxieties to deal with. After seven years of living in New York, we had moved out of our house in Nanuet and were living somewhere near our new house on Warrington Road in Deerfield, Illinois. Construction had been delayed and my parents had not yet moved in, but they were checking on it daily. "This is the finishing work that makes a house a home," my mother wrote. I am sure, with the move, the delay, and the new house, that this was a busy and exhausting time for my father and mother, but I must have pestered my parents to let me see Sputnik 2 and they relented. "Steve has been so interested in the satellite that we promised him we would wake him if it did orbit."

In my imagination they both wake me, my mother nudging me quietly while shushing me so as not to wake my brother, my father standing behind her holding my coat. I rub my eyes awake and see their faces glowing in the half-light of the room, my dad waving us toward the bedroom door. Outside it is cold—this is February, north of Chicago—but it must have been clear. The three of us walk into a grassy clearing away from trees and train our eyes on the evening sky.

Dad lights a cigarette for my mother and then for himself, the glow from the match illuminating their faces against the night sky for a moment like two crescent moons. He shakes out the match and takes a long draw, letting the smoke out slowly. My mother fiddles with her cigarette before taking a quick puff, pulling her coat around her. We wait in the cold briefly, me standing between them, my mother pulling me toward her for warmth.

Suddenly, it appears. "Over there," my dad says, squinting from the smoke, and we turn to face east. The tree line forms a black horizon and above it the Milky Way shimmers in the chilly air.

Dad kneels down, pointing up for me to see. The cigarette at the tips of his fingers traces the arc against the sky. My mother sees it too and, putting an arm on my shoulder, she leans forward to be sure that I have found it. I follow my dad's arm to the spot among the stars and locate it at last, not the satellite itself, which is too small, but the casing, a tiny oblong of light, tumbling silently across the constellations nailed into the night sky. It flip-flops in a regular rhythm, like a heartbeat, without glittering, and, despite its size, glows with a white-bright incandescence. In her letters my mother calls this satellite "Muttnik," a phrase in the press at the time because of the dog inside, but it is hard to think of a dog now, or anything else, living in this slug of pure light.

I cannot imagine that night sky now without creating metaphors from the time three years later that I hid under the stairs and looked at the nails driven into the treads overhead, that coffin-lid of stars that still haunts me as one of the few vivid memories of that time. Thinking of it now, the other memories come flooding back as well. Of me at the top of the stairs watching my mother crying at the kitchen table, while my dad stands off to the side. Of me stepping out of my bedroom to watch my mother sing "Fever" into the record console with a drink in her hand. No, those thoughts, those precious and horrible clues, don't go away, but they also don't erase that night, lost to memory but captured in a letter that I almost didn't read, when my parents and I, somewhere in Illinois, stood in a darkened field together and looked into the heavens. I picture the tableau now like some illustration out of *The Book of Knowledge*, with me standing in my coat and flanked by my parents, my dad pointing and my mother with an arm around me, while the three of us gaze into the night sky with wonder.

"This is," my mother wrote, "a fabulous age."

A Vow of Poverty

In "A Valediction: Forbidding Mourning," John Donne describes those who die so peacefully that mourners, uncertain whether or not the death has happened, begin to argue about it. "As virtuous men pass mildly away," Donne writes, "some of their sad friends" say the "breath goes now, and some say, No." It's a debate that I don't want to hear, thank you—not over *my* dead body!—though I might welcome some comic distraction. I greet warmly the thought of a peaceful death with friends and family gathered, their voices receding all too quickly into the background forever. I'm less anxious about their conversation as we count down my last breaths than I am about the one that will be raging in my own head. Will I, I wonder, lose my nerve?

Writers I admire certainly have. Wallace Stevens, the poet, created a secular paradise out of words and the imagination, but, according to the Archbishop of Hartford, called at his deathbed for a priest. Montaigne, too, asked for last rites at his deathbed after creating a literature in which God is barely mentioned at all. In his writing he claimed that the goal in life is to "take pleasure" and enjoy "true blessings" and "to rest content with them, without any desire to prolong life and reputation." It is a secular vow of poverty, one he broke by calling in a priest to make permanent arrangements for his soul.

So, what about me? During the final flickering of consciousness, will I, too, lose my nerve?

~ ~ ~

The final flickering of consciousness—the thought does give me pause. No one enjoys being awake more than I do. I don't even like to sleep at night. I dread the minutes just before I nod off waiting for somnolence to kick in, and I postpone the ordeal, staying up too late. Counting down to unconsciousness gets to me, the anticipation of "death's second self, that seals up all in rest," and closing my eyes in the dark—the double darkness— gives me the nightly creeps. I am happy the next day when the alarm goes off, though I almost always beat it, and look forward to the glow of window shades in the bedroom signaling that morning has arrived on my porch at last.

Morning rituals please me. My wife and children, who like to sleep, curl up in bedrooms nearby, and I'm comforted by their presence. I pet the dogs who greet me ecstatically, all flapping tails and clattering claws, as if I *had* returned from the dead. After fixing coffee I settle into my chair with a book, the voice of the author clear to me in the quiet just at dawn. I can hear my breathing and feel the beating of my heart in a stillness broken only by the whisper of the turning page. Often I pause for a few minutes to watch the beech tree outside my window fill with light as the sun comes up in its branches. My mind, my first flickering of consciousness, fills with the day as coffee steams beside me.

This cold, January morning is no exception. I start with a few poems while the coffee drips and gurgles. Then I pour myself a cup and settle into a new book, *Credo,* by William Sloane Coffin, "the voice of a prophet and wisdom for the ages," the book jacket says, though I'm having trouble focusing on wisdom just now. Our old dog Chop has risen slowly on her shaky hind legs and hobbled over to me while the little dogs, Madge and Gigi, watch from their pillows. Chop sits in front of me, lifts a paw to the knee of my pajamas, and pants, her tongue lolling on one side of her mouth, her head tilted. *Tilt*, I think with a smile and feel a fresh pang. Her brow furrows expressively, and if she could speak, I know she would. I look into her milky and imploring eyes and realize that the wisdom of the ages may not do the two of us much good, but that this morning, like all my dumpy mornings, is irreplaceable. I wouldn't trade it for the world.

So, what will be on my mind when the last morning comes?

~ ~ ~

I hope my mind does not turn to the usual consolations. The idea that we live on in the thoughts of others is one that brings little comfort. I often think about my friends, but I almost never think about them thinking about me, an eerie notion at best. It would be a static and ultimately rather sad existence, my homunculus peering out from behind the eyes of my wife, my children, and my friends—not to mention my enemies. He would be the recipient of periodic soliloquies, but could never raise his tiny hand to ask a question, crack a new joke, or, for that matter, leave to go to the bathroom. Having given his patrimony away, he would shiver forever in the minds of his children, the rough edges of his personality filed off by the fondling of a loving memory. Freckles and jowls would simply disappear as memories faded, or worse, he might sprout a beard and grow a full head of hair as he becomes confused, over time, with that other guy, what's-his-name. He would never have a new thought and could say nothing except what he is expected to say which is my definition of purgatory. Worst of all, the thought of him gone would prompt grins on the faces of his old foes. I may take pleasure in the notion that others might keep me in mind after I die, entertaining the thought of dear, departed me as they would a guest who has overstayed his welcome, but I would just as soon not try to live there.

The other, more substantial consolation is that death intensifies life and makes it better, a philosophy that works pretty well until we are actually at the point of death and payment for all life's joys is due. "Death is the mother of beauty," wrote Wallace Stevens, the deathbed apostate to our cause. The idea of death generated in him a body of poetry as beautiful as willows that "shiver in the sun" and "new plums and pears" piled on a plate by boys, but, if the archbishop's report is to be believed, it did not help him when the poetry of his life was over. "Without death, we'd never live," writes William Sloane Coffin from my morning reading. "Without discovering the limits of our talents, we'd never discover who we are," the word "limits" smirking euphemistically from his sentence. It is the sum of our disappointments and woes. Once I have come to my limits and reach that chilly bourne where the mind flickers against an endless, icy darkness, I wonder silently as I set my copy of *Credo* down, will I regret that I didn't dwell enough on the subject of my own death?

I hope not.

~ ~ ~

Unfortunately, melancholy oddities crop up and are hard to ignore. Poets, our most honest friends in this business of mortality, take delight, apparently, in pointing them out to us. W. S. Merwin has a poem entitled "For the Anniversary of My Death" in which he draws our attention to the grim fact that each year we pass unremarked the day of our death in much the way that we pass our birthday. In the poem he watches a wren light on a branch, its falling, or perhaps the falling of its song, coming to a stop. After "three days of rain," the wren bobs on the branch, "bowing not knowing to what," as the speaker becomes aware of forces at work in our lives that are beyond our understanding.

In a more recent poem, Billy Collins waxes mathematical, as he attempts to chart the course of our mortal lives, triangulating on the exact moment of death by weighing, emotionally, various pre- and post-mortem indicators. The "Tipping Point" he calls the poem. He begins by noticing that a jazz musician, Eric Dolphy, who had lived for thirty-six years, has been dead for thirty-six years as well, and wonders if anyone else had noticed the strange fact that the world had taken another "full Dolphy step forward in time," that it had "flipped over the Eric Dolphy yardstick once again?" After pondering this oddity, Collins wonders if his own life has reached a tipping point. Were he to flip the yardstick of the life he has lived so far, would the end match up with the day of his demise? It had been raining, he explains, and he felt a "little shift" a moment before when he checked the mail. It would be "subtle" the poet admits, "as you passed through... the exact center of your life," perhaps like crossing "the equator at night in a boat," but certainly someone as sensitive as a poet would *feel* the tipping point.

The question I want to ask our poets is whether a *memento mori* based on something as abstract as the calendar requires a rainy day? Isn't it likely that the rain, and the emotions created by rain, got to them both? Who can blame Merwin for thinking way ahead? Three days of rain will do that to you, taking your eye off of the present joys and calamities of the world. As for listening to jazz on rainy days—even a light-hearted poet like Billy Collins knows that's a mistake, the melody line of life lost in a sad trickle of harmonic possibilities. We feel nothing unusual, of course, at the anniversary of our deaths or the exact center of our lives and *that* is the real point of these poems. We pass through those ethereal foreshadowings blithely unaware of our doom, in the same way that we, despite our poets, live the other days of our lives. It is a blessing. Each day swells of its own accord in the nectar of our indifference, ordinariness hemming us in on all sides, crowding out morbidity. Life, it seems, delivers up its joys more honestly when thoughts of death recede and we take our time on earth for granted, when mornings stretch endlessly before us like a summer beach. We don't need evenings to enjoy the plump middle of our days.

~ ~ ~

Eventually, though, evening comes and our losses add up, casting our former joys in a dimmer light. Sometimes, in the gloom, I don't recognize myself. Lately Barbara has renamed our dogs Tilt, Tripod, and Trouble. Tripod is a high-strung, black-and-white rat terrier with a brown chin and very delicate legs whose real name is Madge. A snarling red yard dog in the neighborhood attacked her several months ago, ripping her open and breaking her hind paw. Now she gets along on three legs and often stands, gazing up at us like a tripod. Later we discovered that the instigator of the dog fight was not the red dog—the instrument of death we had groused indignantly—but our own, newly acquired pound puppy, Gigi, who likes to charge up our neighbor's hill, bringing on the attack. So, we call her Trouble.

But the dog that breaks our hearts is our old stray, Chop, a beautiful mixed breed that looks like a cross between a golden lab and an Irish setter. We have had her ever since 1991, the miracle year when the

Atlanta Braves rose from last place to first in one season, and named her after the infamous, and we belatedly realized offensive, salute that fans make during the games, the tomahawk chop. Two weeks ago she suffered a blow. My daughter, Alice, found her in a room downstairs lying in her own vomit and urine and unable to walk. The vet treated her for an inner ear infection, but when that medicine didn't work, he said that she probably had suffered a stroke. We had to decide if we should put her down or not, the vet explaining that our choice was a "quality of life issue."

Quality of life—how can a person decide that for a dog? Clearly the stroke was hard. The right side of her body is weak, one eye droops, half-closed, and her head perpetually tilts. At first, when she started walking again, she limped in circles until she managed to compensate for the weak side, and even now she stumbles at times when she turns left. She can't make right turns at all and has to go around the front of the porch when we call her for her food. But she eats well, has no pain as far as I can tell, and wags her tail happily when any of us enters the room or calls her name. When I walk her through the neighborhood, she zigzags a little but holds her nose to the wind and her tail high. Head on, she looks a little goofy, as if, Barbara says, she is looking around the corner—except that there is no corner. Still, she seems unembarrassed by her appearance. In fact, it is amazing to me that a dog can lose half its mind and still function so well. Quality of life, who knows? As Barbara points out, it is not as if she read the classics before.

Still, on a morning like this one, I can't help but register the loss, as Chop struggles to rise and walk over to me. She seems happy enough as I rub her ears and run my hand along her neck, but every wag of the tail or lifting of the paw, the signals in her world of greeting, now has a valedictory feel. Summer afternoons on the porch when Chop was a healthy young dog, she would sometimes lower her head and look at us imploringly, on the verge, it seemed, of speech, and we thought the gesture was her way of joining in on the happy conversation. Now her inquisitive look is involuntary and on this January morning in my living room, the paw on my knee and cockeyed look of her face convey sadness. I wonder if, from the beginning, she had been saying goodbye.

~ ~ ~

The poet Elizabeth Bishop identifies the "One Art" we all must master in life as the "art of losing." When we misplace our car keys or lose our place in a book, we are simply practicing for the big one. Wallace Stevens in "Waving Adieu, Adieu, Adieu," one of the finest of his short, little-known poems, writes that in a world without an afterlife the endings in our lives would be true endings, not partings. Each happy moment contains its own goodbye. "Just to be there," he writes, "would be bidding farewell." He repeats the phrase, "bidding farewell," as if he is continuously waving goodbye, and explains, poignantly, that one "likes to practice the thing."

Poets come rushing in on this point. In his sequence "Dark Harbor," Mark Strand, making a striking allusion to Stevens, reminds us that practice at saying goodbye is not really necessary at all. Each moment is elegiac no matter what we do. Whether we cry or wave or look away "it is still farewell. Farewell no matter what." We do not just practice loss, we enact it continuously, like Wallace Stevens' automaton waving slowly forever. Sensual moments—watching pelicans dive in the lagoon, say, or bathers at the beach—only accentuate the loss, turning being itself into "an occasion for mourning." Unlike the Billy Collins' *memento mori* of the calendar, we can register this feeling *De Profundis*. We are apt to feel impending doom most when we seize a moment and, satiated, enjoy its fullness: when the moon waxes, when the wine is poured, or, most poignantly, when we grow sleepy. No music, no poetry, can change our condition. Every hello is a goodbye.

~ ~ ~

But is that true? Does the muse so relentlessly dog our joyous days?

At the end of her life, my grandmother had an irritating habit of answering each choice with the phrase, "that'll be fine." Do you want to hear some music or watch TV, Grandma? That'll be fine. Do you want to go to Glen Elder this morning or drive by the farm? That'll be fine. Do you want me to drive the car into Waconda Lake or head-on into a Mack truck? Fine. Does everyone in Kansas talk this way? Maybe it is a part of their innate sense of modesty. Who knows? Living under a big sky where the view in every direction looks about the same might make choosing seem pointless. North or South? That'll be fine.

I think it was her way of not saying goodbye.

Grandma knew a lot about goodbye. Her daughter—my mother and her only child—committed suicide. Her husband died soon after from grief. My brother and I—her "boys"—were her pride and joy, though we were too shell-shocked by family life to be very responsive. Most of her long letters to us after the death of our mother went unanswered, even, I'm ashamed to say, when they contained money. She remarried late in life, to a happy-go-lucky sportswriter named Raleigh. He had been an old flame, her first true love, and I think that she was happier then than I had ever known her to be, but he died of emphysema a few years later. She and Raleigh liked to play a board game with marbles, and he would crack jokes making Grandma laugh so hard the table shook. Once, I recall, Raleigh laughed so hard he started coughing and had to be hooked up to oxygen.

"That would be waving," Wallace Stevens wrote, "and meaning farewell."

Grandma was beautiful as a girl with an angelic face. In her youthful pictures she looks wispy and romantic. As she got older, she grew portly, and I always remember her as soft and round. She loved to eat out, usually at the local cafés, and found the opening of a new one as cause to celebrate. After Raleigh died her social life revolved around eating out with friends from church, and when we visited, we went out to eat every night. Kansas is one of those places that likes to name its restaurants after highways, so we'd ask, Grandma, do you want to eat at Wendy's or the 24/66?

That'll be fine.

The word "fine" means, among other things, "the end." We hear it in "finite" and see it as the last word in some old books. I first heard the word used that way by my grandfather who ended his recitation of the months of the year with these lines:

> February has twenty-eight days in fine
> Till leap year gives it twenty nine.

If you asked my grandmother—at any moment of her life—how she was doing she would, like most Kansans, answer "fine," and she meant it, resigning herself to all her endings, I'm convinced, even on terrible days. It was a coda to a lifetime of loses.

But the word "fine" means more than just the end. When the waitress at the 24/66 offers a chess pie dessert, and we are full, we raise our open hands in the air and say, "No, I'm fine." Not only am I done, but I'm okay with that. We may feel a pang of regret as the waitress cocks an eyebrow and glares at us over her pad with that are-you-sure look on her face, but if we are mature, we can muster up the moxie to insist: "I'm fine." I've had enough. Each hello may contain a goodbye, as the poets insist, but every wave that bids adieu displays an open palm.

No, I'm fine.

~ ~ ~

It's time for me to take a vow of poverty. The traditional vow requires that we ask less of life and await heavenly rewards, but I am profligate of mornings and happily squander them, so that will not work. If one life is all I have, then I'll insist on having it all. My goal is to get lost in my days, enjoying most of them by taking them for granted. They may be gods, as Emerson wrote, but they are shy divinities. Knowing that living happens in the present, I aim to be a connoisseur of the plain in uncommon light. Like a scientist, I'll direct the microscopic lens of my pen on a moment and adjust the mirror. Whether it rains or not, I can find no footing in heaven— it is too ethereal and empty for me—but at the tip of a dripping leaf, I hang on a bead of forever available only in the here and now.

My vow of poverty is to demand one lifetime and nothing more. On my deathbed I ask for the courage to accept the simple truth: I've had enough. I do not want to be worn down by life—to have had enough because I'm beaten by illness, old age, and the loss of loved ones—though that will in all likelihood happen, offering a clue to the proper response to death. No, I hope I've had enough because I have had my full share.

That is what I say now, but what will I be thinking when the doctor leans over me to check my breathing one last time. Will I have second thoughts? I probably will feel a pang as the lights of consciousness flicker, and I pass a slab of pie from the waitress's hand to some other customer in the 24/66 that is our café at the crossroads here on earth. I have so much to give away, beginning with a beech tree, three damaged dogs, and the dross of all of those waking hours I've happily burned through over a lifetime. So, to renew my vow I practice the thing each morning. As I write in silence, I listen to my breathing and recall the throb of my heartbeat, sounds present with me in my mother's womb that will ring in my ears on my deathbed. They could be construed as my first living utterances, and, regardless of my dying recantations, they will be my last words. After a lifetime of listening, I can translate their double thump and wheeze. The sibilant breath whispers "yes," and the limping two-syllable beat of the heart says "I'm fine" over and over, till the end.

"I'm fine, yes. I'm fine. Yes, I'm fine."

KINDLY DARK

John Shook stood in the parking lot looking up at the evening sky. He had sheet music under one arm and wore a buttoned-down shirt, a breeze lifting the blond hair from his forehead. This was exam time, and he had no doubt just left a juried performance in the music building. Now he stood relaxed, all the tension of the day having drained from him. I had come from the Humanities building in a hurry and probably a little frazzled, a stack of papers under my arm, apprehensive about the long night of grading ahead. But when I saw him there, I stopped too, taken, I suppose, by his calm, and looked up, wondering what had caught his attention. It was the sky. The orange on the underside of the clouds had retreated to the horizon, glowing like embers along the ridge tops, igniting the mountains and leaving behind an evening dome of dusky and deepening purple. We stood side by side— man and boy—and watched silently from different spots on the asphalt.

"It's getting kindly dark," he said at last, squinting. Then he turned to me and smiled.

"Kindly dark" is a mountain phrase, and John, one of the sweet-faced boys from the Shook family, has no doubt heard it all of his life. The Shooks were among the first whites to arrive in our area of the southern Appalachians after the Cherokee were forcibly removed in the 1830s, and they, and their relatives, have settled in the hills and coves all around the school where I teach English. As part of the seventeenth- and eighteenth-century wave of immigrants from the British Isles, their language is

Elizabethan in character, and, when their guard is down and they can speak freely, it is lovely to hear.

A friend once asked if it hurt my ears to teach English in Appalachia. She thought, I suppose, that I spent my days on the prowl for grammar errors and must be offended by double negatives and verbs that fail to agree with their subjects. "Their language is *my* teacher," I explained. "If I listen hard enough, I always learn something new from it." To tell the truth, I enjoy it, though many mountain people, knowing what I do for a living, try their best to hide the way they speak from me. When John looked up at the evening sky and said "kindly dark," it was like spotting a rare bird. Amid mountains bearing the burden of the day's dying light, a seventeen-year-old boy offered up Shakespearean wisdom. It was a privilege to be there.

I have always loved late evening, the twilight hour when the day relinquishes its bustle to the power of night. It is the in-between time when all is in a state of transformation from clarity to obscurity, and nothing is as it seems. The Celtic forbears of John and the other Shooks considered the hours of twilight magical as well, a liminal time when the world as we know it gives way to the world of dreams—and nightmares. No doubt apprehensions sweep over us if we pay attention to this shift, the earth turning its mighty bulk away from the sun and facing off into endless space. Even in the placid little parking-lot tableau of evening, I'm anxious and John is squinting, his brow wrinkled. This hour is beautiful, yes, but by its very nature it is also gloomy and a little weird. The phrase, coming naturally to John's lips, brings with it comfort in this twilight, a hint of welcome from the unknown: "It's getting *kindl*y dark."

When I moved to the mountains Barbara and I liked to take our walk at twilight, shedding our daily selves by immersing them in the poetry of the hour. At that time, the maintenance building at the edge of the campus had a tall, unused chimney that rose against the horizon, and each evening as the sky turned murky, a flock of swifts rose in consort like a jotted line, fluttered momentarily against the bruise-blue sky, and suddenly, as if on cue, tumbled into the sooty chimney for the night. We often stopped to watch, taking comfort at the daring of the birds and their concerted descent into darkness. After the maintenance chimney was torn down, releasing the swifts from their nightly obsession, I often liked to walk to the end of my driveway to watch night fall over the mountains seeing in memory the calligraphy of birds punctuating the smudgy horizon.

I'm reminded of that other mountain phrase for evening, one full of the beauty and foreboding of the hour: *dusky dark*. Why is that phrase so beguiling? Perhaps it is the alliteration on the "d" sounds or repeated "k's" though I'm distrustful of such a reading since it draws on my background as an English teacher, and a technical discussion like that rarely tricks out the real power of this language. I sense something unnamable and more important happening with the vowels—the "u" and "ar" sound coming from the same deep part of the throat, the pure "u" giving way to the guttural "r". It is not completely dark, the phrase tells us, a hint of light remains glittering along those repeated consonants, but the light *is* fading, the vowels growl, and will not return until black night is done with us. I'm reminded that this area of the Appalachian hills was one of the last regions of the United States to acquire electrical power. When night fell in that earlier time, it fell hard, the enormous darkness of the cosmos held back by little more than kerosene lamps. For many of John's ancestors, the phrase "dusky dark" meant smoky chimneys, bears and bats, and the howls of painters that roamed the hills nocturnally.

Even for those of us who have plenty of electrical light, the evening can bring with it weariness, if not dread. I grow weary as I grade, I know. Many of my colleagues get upset about errors in the papers of the young, but to be frank, that is not what bothers me. Finding errors gives me a sense of job security, and I *will* get worried when they disappear. What drags me down—as the evening falls away to the dead of night and the lamp glows over my shoulder—is the predictability of my responses to mistakes that are brand new to them. I jot the same symbol beside a comma splice that I wrote thirty years ago, a slash through the comma followed by 'cs' off to the side. "Develop this idea more fully," I write often on every set of papers, clinging to the edge of their silences with well-worn exasperation. "Cut!" I exclaim, though the redundancy is mine. When I grade papers, I am grading myself, and my stinginess with "A's" marks the distance I'll never cover. The edge foolish youth has on us, I realize as I jam the papers in my briefcase late at night and turn out the light, is eternal foolishness.

My own writing brings with it the same burden. I do this work at dawn, the other twilight hour of the day, and often when I begin it is still dark outside. I think of Yeats in his tower and Dante climbing stairs during his lonely exile as I make my way down in darkness to the windowless study in my basement. In this business, it is smart to be in good company, and here, I am. Before me, I face an empty computer screen, but at my back, I have the accumulated whispers of a wall full of books, and we have been at this a long time. Is it a good sign that every essay I write feels like the last? I doubt it. Will we ever find words to fill the void? Despite his brilliance, Dante left enough darkness for Shakespeare to fill. Zora Neale Hurston did not shut up Alice Walker. We have plenty of void to pass around, it seems. What dusky dark waits for us there? Who knows? We may throw a lifetime of words against the dark and empty sky, and we'll never come to terms with it.

But the phrase, "kindly dark," offers some relief from all this murk. John probably means "kind *of*" when he says "kind*ly*," but his wording inevitably drags other associations with it. "Kindly" has come to mean genially or benignly as in the happy line from the Robert Burns' poem, "Bessy and Her Spinning Wheel," written in 1792 that says the "sun blinks kindly in the beil," but this meaning of the word is relatively recent. In its original sense it meant "in accordance with nature" and is related to words such as "kin" and "kindred." Used this way, the word kindly means "in a manner appropriate to the nature of the thing." Natural and fitting as opposed to forced, imposed, or artificial—that is the older meaning of the word that I hear in John's mountain phrase. "Crabs will kindly crawl or crepe," one text from Shakespeare's time explains, and Phillip Sidney, in *Arcadia* writes, that when we want to open a conversation, we should wait until "there might kindly arise a fit beginning." It is with this meaning of the word that kindness yields to wisdom. The thought that the end of the day—even an exam day—is not only friendly but also fitting is a comfort. It shakes my gloom, and the somber pages that I have hauled with me all my adult life glow like the rising moon with a borrowed light.

The dark is kindly because it is appropriate to the nature of our lives. We knew it before we were born and when we close our eyes it is there, where it always lurks. Sometimes, when we sing, laugh, and make love we do just that, don't we—we close our eyes? He who would know the road, St. John of the Cross says somewhere in one of those books at my back, must close his eyes and learn how to walk in the dark. I carry this wisdom in my body and it generates the pages I hold in my hands. I'm not sure what I said to John Shook before he and I went our separate ways. No doubt I looked up too at the darkening sky while our shadows lengthened and faded on the asphalt behind us. I know that the phrase brought a smile to my lips. This thing of darkness, Prospero says of Caliban, I acknowledge mine. The dark kindly suits us. In the blink of an eye, it comes.

GRATITUDE

My Beloved Republic is large, and I have many people to thank beginning with writer and editor Joe Mackall, to whom I owe my whole career, and my close writer friends Robert Root and Kathy Winograd. These three were there at the creation of most of these essays and sustained me with their intelligence, good cheer, and kindness. Many others pitched in with friendship, comments, advice, and support including Scott Russell Sanders, Michael Steinberg, Jocelyn Bartkevicius, Jill Christman, Mark Neely, Sonya Huber, Bonnie Rough, Bob Cowser, Tom Larson, Dan Lehman, Enid Shomer, Richard Hoffman, Stephen Haven, Leila Philip, Ruth Schwartz, Rebecca McClanahan, Patrick Madden, Sue Silverman, Robert Atwan, Cheryl Strayed, Mimi Schwartz, Kate Hopper, Dinty Moore, Judith Kitchen, Stan Rubin, Rosemary Royston, Jan Shoemaker, Sarah Wells, Jeremy Collins, Josette Kubaszyk, Kate Carroll de Gutes, Brenda Miller, Sandra Swinburne, Heather Weber, Tarn Wilson, Denise Wilkinson, John Kay, David W. Fenza, John Lane, Bettie Sellers, and Janice Moore.

I am indebted to my publisher, Jill McCabe Johnson, and the wonderful community of writers and editors at The Wandering Aengus Press for selecting my book for the nonfiction prize. Jill's vision of "publishing works to enrich lives and make the world a better place" sets her publishing enterprises squarely in the Beloved Republic. I especially thank my editor, Ana Maria Spagna, for her friendship and superb suggestions which made my book more intimate and focused.

I have had much support from the many writers and readers I met on-line as part of The Humble Essayist website including Sarah Einstein,

Jill Talbot, Sonja Livingston, Amy Wright, Mary Woster Haug, Philip Weinstein, Anne McGrath, and Annie Dawid.

I also thank Young Harris College and the Ashland University MFA Program where I worked while writing most of these essays as well as the many colleagues and friends there. Thanks go as well to artist Dale Cochran, who has an eye for beauty, and Jennifer and Don Cordier, and Brenda Hull who are part of my musical group, Butternut Creek and Friends, who find peace in harmony.

My Beloved Republic includes writers that I know only from their books—many of them included in this collection—and I thank them too.

Finally, my Beloved Republic includes my family and friends who wander in and out of these pages at various times of their lives. At the center of it all, raising high the pennant of the Republic of Love, is my wife and best friend, Barbara.

ACKNOWLEDGMENTS

The author wishes to thank the following publications in which these essays originally appeared, often in different form. These magazines kept this work alive until it found final book form.

Another Chicago Magazine: "Madre Luz"

American Literary Review: "One Boy's Luminous Skin"

Antioch Review: "The Beloved Republic"

Ascent: "Blood Mountain"

Banjo Newsletter: "Gatherin' around J.P. Fraley"

Best American Essays 2013: "The Book of Knowledge"

Best American Essays 2018: "The Other Steve Harvey"

Brevity: "A Whole Life"

Hotel America: "Orphaned Souls"

Michigan Quarterly Review: "The Other Steve Harvey"

River Teeth: "A Laying on of Hands," "The Book of Knowledge," "Ya Mismo," and "Kindly Dark"

Solstice: "The Arc of the Universe" as "The Arc of the Moral Universe"

The Florida Review: "A Vow of Poverty"

The Hopkins Review: "The Razor Blade"

About the Author

Steven Harvey is the author of *The Book of Knowledge and Wonder*, a memoir about coming to terms with the suicide of his mother, published by Ovenbird Books as part of the "Judith Kitchen Select" series. He is the author of a book-length essay, *Folly Beach*, and three collections of personal essays: *A Geometry of Lilies*, *Lost in Translation*, and *Bound for Shady Grove*. In addition, he edited an anthology of essays written by men on middle age called *In a Dark Wood*. Two of his essays have been selected for *The Best American Essays*: "The Book of Knowledge" in 2013 and "The Other Steve Harvey" in 2018. Over the years, fifteen of his essays have been recognized as notable by that series as well, and he was twice honored as a finalist in the Associated Writing Program's nonfiction contest. He is a professor emeritus of English and creative writing at Young Harris College, a founding faculty member in the Ashland University MFA program in creative writing, a contributing editor for *River Teeth* magazine, and the creator of The Humble Essayist, a website designed to promote literary nonfiction. He lives with his wife in the north Georgia mountains where he sings and plays banjo, guitar, and ukulele in the folk group Butternut Creek and Friends. You can learn about Steve and his work, and see photos, videos and more about this book, at his web site: www.steven-harvey-author.com.